AN INTRODUCTION
TO THE ARCHITECTURAL
HERITAGE *of*

COUNTY WICKLOW

AN ROINN COMHSHAOIL, OIDHREACHTA AGUS RIALTAIS ÁITIÚIL
DEPARTMENT OF THE ENVIRONMENT, HERITAGE
AND LOCAL GOVERNMENT

Foreword

County Wicklow has an architectural heritage as rich and diverse as its contrasting landscapes. The large country houses at Kilrudderry, Powerscourt and Russborough, the fine Georgian merchant town houses in Arklow, the small estate houses in Stratford and Shillelagh, and vernacular structures like the Dwyer-McAllister cottage at Derrynamuck, all bear witness to the complexity of the county's social structure and its changing patterns of settlement.

The Military Road and its associated barracks mark the troubled history of the county and its strategic relationship to Dublin. The monastic site at Glendalough is one of the most noted religious complexes in the country. The many churches of all denominations throughout the county continue a building tradition over fifteen hundred years old. With its timber and granite, Wicklow had building materials at its doorstep. The quarry at Ballyknockan supplied granite for many of the county's prominent buildings, as well as to the distinctive stone-cutters' village of Ballyknockan itself.

The fieldwork carried out by the NIAH in the summer of 2003 covers approximately twelve hundred sites, structures or groups of structures. Wicklow's county town, Wicklow, is not included, as it was previously recorded in the separate Wicklow Town Survey published in 1997. Nevertheless some structures of special interest in the town have been alluded to in the following text. The purpose of the NIAH survey and the Introduction is to identify and highlight a representative selection of the architectural heritage of County Wicklow. It is hoped that through raising awareness, a better appreciation will be encouraged, together with a drive to protect the county's significant built heritage.

The NIAH survey of the architectural heritage of County Wicklow can be accessed on the Internet at:
www.buildingsofireland.ie

NATIONAL INVENTORY
of ARCHITECTURAL HERITAGE

**COUNTY WICKLOW
(c. 1850)**

This mid nineteenth-century 'panoramic view' effectively illustrates the extent of the mountainous interior of County Wicklow and the relative closeness of this, for many centuries largely inaccessible, area to Dublin.

Courtesy of the National Library of Ireland.

Introduction

Wicklow is a maritime county located in the east of Ireland. Bordered by County Dublin in the north, Kildare and Carlow in the west, and Wexford in the south, Wicklow takes its name from the county town, which is believed to derive from the Norse 'Uíkar-ló' or 'Meadow of the Bay'. Its Irish name, Cill Mhantain, 'Mantan's church', derives from a follower of Saint Patrick, said to have founded a church near Black Castle. Of all of the Leinster counties, Wicklow is among the most physically diverse. Although popularly known as the 'Garden of Ireland' it in fact contains a number of contrasting landscapes, from the long fertile low lying coastal strip to the east, to the extensive mountainous mass of the centre, and the more gentle rolling hills of the south and south west. The mountains are undoubtedly the county's most spectacular feature, forming the largest unbroken highland area in the country, and containing Lugnaquilla (925 metres), the second highest peak in the land. They are rugged in places, and interspersed with dramatic picturesque glens, loughs, and rivers. To the south and far west the landscape of rich pastureland, farms, and scattered towns and villages, has much in common with the neighbouring counties of Kildare, Carlow, and Wexford. The more populous east, with its string of relatively large coastal towns – Bray, Greystones, Wicklow, and Arklow – is in many respects a continuation of the highly developed coast of south County Dublin. Wicklow is the most densely wooded county in Ireland and can boast the country's highest waterfall, Powerscourt; the highest village, Roundwood; and the two highest mountain passes, the Sally Gap and the Wicklow Gap.

VALE ROAD
Arklow
(c. 1830)

A collection of small-scale
early nineteenth-century
terraced houses of some
vernacular quality form
an appealing uniform
streetscape pattern in the
centre of Arklow.

RATHDRUM CORN MILL
Low Street,
Rathdrum
(c. 1860)

Wicklow's many rivers
historically encouraged
the establishment of mill
complexes across the
county. The mill at
Rathdrum, dating to the
mid nineteenth century,
supported much of the
local agricultural economy
and was an important
centre for the processing
of corn.

This varied landscape has shaped the development of the county. The east was prone to successive waves of settlers, among them the Vikings who gave the county its first recognisable towns of Wicklow and Arklow. The Normans and the English followed, and the eastern part of the county consequently witnessed a much greater degree of urbanisation than the higher ground, which preserved its Gaelic culture until the early seventeenth century and proved a largely inaccessible region right up until the early 1800s. The proximity to the capital of what was a remote and frequently lawless area has also proved important. Much of the history of sixteenth-century Wicklow, culminating with the shiring of the county in 1606, can be explained in terms of Tudor and Stuart attempts to come to terms with this. It also explains why a military road was built straight through the mountains in the wake of the 1798 Rebellion. On a more peaceful note, the closeness of this mountainous range to Dublin made it an ideal site for the large reservoirs that were built to serve the growing metropolis in the late nineteenth and early twentieth centuries; the Vartry Reservoir, Roundwood, was created in the 1860s and the

Pollaphuca Reservoir, Blessington, in the 1930s. Granite from the same Wicklow hills was used in the construction of many of Dublin's finest buildings, and, more mundanely, put to use as the capital's kerbstones! Granite has proven to be one of Wicklow's enduring natural resources. During the seventeenth and early eighteenth centuries the county's wealth of timber also proved of great value. Oak was used not only in ship and house building, but also in the tanning and iron industries. Later, in the nineteenth century, the area's ample deposits of minerals, including copper, lead, iron, and gold, were to lead to the employment of thousands at the mines in Avoca, Glenmalure, and Luganure. By this time, and rather in contrast to the unsightly mining sites, Wicklow's greatest resource, the landscape itself, was attracting myriads of tourists. Its picturesque and evocative qualities greatly appealed to the Romantic sensibilities of the age. Today, this landscape, now readily accessible and minus many of its former industries, continues to attract many thousands each year, its delightful wooded glens and vast tracts of rugged unspoilt hills appealing to the tourist and the filmmaker in search of an evocative timeless backdrop.

VIEW OF POWER-SCOURT, COUNTY WICKLOW
(c. 1760-2)

Executed by George the Elder Barret (1728-84), this landscape view of Powerscourt House illustrates the dramatic backdrop presented by the Sugar Loaf Mountain, into which the estate gardens, originally landscaped by Richard Castle and subsequently redeveloped, appear to merge.

Courtesy of Yale Center for British Art, Paul Melon Collection, USA/Bridgeman Art Library.

POWERSCOURT HOUSE
Powerscourt Demesne Enniskerry
(1731-40)

The gardens at Powerscourt rival the house itself in terms of beauty. They were redesigned in the mid nineteenth century by the 6th and 7th Viscounts Powerscourt, largely to designs drawn up by the architect Daniel Robertson (fl. 1812-49).

Pre 1700

Wicklow has been a place of human habitation since Neolithic times, and the less mountainous areas of the county are rich in prehistoric, Early Christian and medieval sites. Most of the built structures which have survived reflect the dominance of military, defensive, and religious matters, both pre-Christian and Christian, in life throughout all of these eras. One of the most impressive sites belonging to the former category is the 10.5 hectare late Bronze Age hilltop fortress of Rathcoran, to the north of Baltinglass, where remains include a double set of ramparts and a chambered cairn. There is a similarly large fort at Rathgall, near Wicklow town, with dry stone walls that encompass an area of roughly 308 metres in diameter and include an inner enclosure of about 46 metres. The best known of the religious sites, both locally and nationally, is the collection of buildings at Glendalough *(fig. 1)*. This monastic settlement, reputedly founded by Saint Kevin in the late sixth or early seventh century, in an idyllic but typically remote setting, was much in tune with the ascetic ethos of the early church in Ireland. The site as we see it today largely consists of eighth- to twelfth-century remains. Among the most impressive of these is the cathedral dedicated to Saint Peter and Saint Paul; a multi-period structure with a tenth-century nave and a chancel of the late 1100s. Also of note are the distinctive, but erroneously named, 'Saint Kevin's Kitchen', a two-storey twelfth-century oratory with a round tower-like belfry, and the

30.5 metre high 'round tower', re-roofed in 1876. The gatehouse at the eastern entrance to the settlement is the only surviving example of its type in the country.

The buildings at Glendalough, with their simple rectangular plans, steeply pitched roofs, and general lack of decoration, are all very typical of the early and in many respects insular Irish church. Things began to change in the 1100s when the church was gradually brought more closely in line with the Continental model, entailing the introduction of new religious orders that brought new forms of architecture in their wake. This is clearly seen in the remnants of the Cistercian abbey of Vallis Salutis or 'Valley of Health' at Baltinglass. Founded in 1148 by Dermot McMurrough, King of Leinster, this site has a more rigidly planned layout of cruciform church with cloister, chapter house, and refectory. This layout, as well as its Romanesque detailing, is in keeping with other such houses elsewhere in the British Isles and Continental Europe. It is worth noting that the detailing employs the simpler motifs that are a particularly Irish characteristic.

Dermot McMurrough's dealings with the Anglo-Normans and their subsequent settlement in the east of Wicklow, together with much of the east and south of Ireland, led directly to the introduction of another Continental building form; the castle. Many were built by followers of the Anglo-Norman leader, Strongbow. Dating from the late 1100s,

(fig. 1)
GLENDALOUGH
(c. 700-c. 1100)

A group of buildings dating
to a period spanning four
centuries form an extensive
ecclesiastical complex with
origins dating to the sixth
or seventh century. The
slender round tower rises
above the surrounding
landscape and has become
an internationally-recognised
symbol of the built heritage
of County Wicklow.

*Courtesy of the Photographic
Unit, Department of the
Environment, Heritage
and Local Government.*

Black Castle, a triangular keep commenced by Maurice Fitzgerald on a rocky headland just south east of Wicklow harbour, is one of the earliest castles to appear in the county. Part of a south-west tower and a section of the south-east wall of the castle itself still survive. Theobald Walter erected a similar stronghold at the county's other major urban settlement of Arklow around the same time; the strategically important lands in the north of the county, neighbouring Dublin, were protected by the Great Castle at Bray, built by Walter de Ridlesford. Initially, many of these structures would have consisted of simple keeps and out-

buildings, all constructed in timber and surrounded by a timber palisade; the timber structures were later replaced with stone. Such sturdy edifices helped protect the nascent Anglo-Norman colony in Wicklow and were a highly visible sign of the power of the English crown. Manorial economies developed around many of them, existing towns such as Arklow and Wicklow expanded, and new settlements began to emerge, like Bray and Newcastle. Matters were sufficiently peaceful by the early fourteenth century to allow the appearance of a more domesticated form of castle, the two-storey hall-house, such as that at Kindlestown.

(fig. 2)
KILTIMON CASTLE
Dunran Demesne,
Newcastle
(c. 1550)

With its simple square plan and lack of adornment, Kiltimon is typical of the many tower houses constructed during late medieval and Tudor times. The corner bartizans, however, are fanciful late Georgian additions.

(fig. 3)
CARNEW CASTLE
Main Street,
Carnew
(c. 1590)

Despite its origins as a garrison, Carnew Castle was described in 1625 as 'a well contrived and convenient house'. It was burnt in the Rebellion of 1641, and again in the 1798 Rebellion. The building was repaired and 'Georgianised' by Earl Fitzwilliam (c. 1817).

(fig. 4)
CARNEW CASTLE
Main Street,
Carnew

An ogee-headed carriageway introduces an elegant quality to an otherwise utilitarian structure in the grounds of Carnew Castle.

(fig. 5)
POWERSCOURT HOUSE
Powerscourt Demesne,
Enniskerry
(1731-40)

Richard Castle (1690-1751)
settled in Ireland around
1728 and worked initially
with Sir Edward Lovett
Pearce (c. 1699-1733).
After the latter's death in
1733, Castle became the
foremost architect in the
country and was responsi-
ble for some of the finest
mansions of the period.
Powerscourt House, built
enveloping a fourteenth-
century tower house, is
considered one of his
greatest achievements.

BALLYMURRIN HOUSE
Ballymurrin Lower,
Kilbride
(c. 1675)

Ballymurrin House is an
extremely rare example of
a pre-1700s dwelling of
the 'middling' sort. It was
built by a Quaker family
called Pym, and in com-
mon with many other
Quaker houses, is believed
to have been used for
holding religious meetings
also. The slightly lower
section to the south is an
addition, said to have
been built as two
dwellings for the daugh-
ters of the original owner.

With the waning of the Crown's influence after the mid 1300s de facto power fell into the hands of local lords, of both Gaelic and settler descent, who erected that particularly Irish form of private castle, the tower house, to protect their own territories and to launch attacks on rivals. Of these, notable examples are to be found at Kiltimon (c. 1550) *(fig. 2)* and Threecastles (c. 1500), whilst present country houses such as Killruddery (originally c. 1550 and 1652) and Powerscourt (originally c. 1300) *(fig. 5)* either incorporate, or stand on sites previously occupied by such buildings. Most tower houses were tall, stark structures, generally with four storeys over a tall ground floor level, and an overall emphasis on verticality. The well preserved, though somewhat Georgianised, late sixteenth-century Carnew Castle (c. 1590) is a variation on the tower house theme *(figs. 3-4)*. Unlike most others,

however, Carnew was built by Crown forces rather than by a semi-independent local lord. With the shiring of Wicklow in 1606 the county was in theory finally brought completely under Crown control. The decades that followed, however, were just as unsettled as those preceding. As the fortified house at Killincarrig (c. 1625) demonstrates, architecture remained largely defensive rather than domestic in nature. Castles and tower houses continued to be occupied, while many churches and religious buildings, destroyed in the upheavals that followed the Reformation (1645-9) and the Williamite Wars (1659-91), were not repaired. By the closing years of the century more settled conditions were to lead to the beginnings of a transformation in the built landscape of Wicklow in which domestic, rather than defensive or religious, structures were to predominate.

The Eighteenth Century

With the ending of the Williamite Wars, County Wicklow, like the rest of the Kingdom of Ireland, entered an era of comparative political calm which was to last, without interruption, for over a century. This tranquillity engendered a period of building which was to transform the face of the county. Central to this transformation were the county's major landowners who, secure in their positions, commenced the building of new mansions. Without the need to refer to defensive matters, they were able to begin experimenting with the latest styles of architecture, as well as fostering the expansion of their estate towns and villages and, in some cases, laying out new settlements. To a certain degree, the beginnings of this change in the built landscape were apparent before the late 1690s, during the relatively peaceful period following the Restoration (c. 1660-85). In 1673 the Archbishop of Dublin and Lord Chancellor of Ireland, Michael Boyle (c. 1609-1702), began to build a large two-storey H-plan mansion at Blessington. The building, now demolished, had a grand colonnaded entrance and a hipped roof with dormered attic storey. Shortly thereafter, Boyle laid out the present town and built the church. Around the same date the Kennedys erected a large mansion house at Mount Kennedy. The Earl of Meath's house at Kilruddery, near Bray, is also seventeenth century in origin, as is Ballyarthur (c. 1680), near Woodenbridge *(fig. 6)*. Kilruddery was greatly extended and remodelled in an Elizabethan Revival manner in the 1820s. Ballyarthur's late seventeenth-century form, with five-bay front and steeply pitched hipped roof, is still apparent despite a reworking of the front façade in the early 1800s.

(fig. 6)
BALLYARTHUR HOUSE
Ballyarthur,
Woodenbridge
(c. 1680)

The late seventeenth-century origins of Ballyarthur House are clearly expressed in the breakfront through the tight grouping of the openings. Originally built for the Bayly family, the house was entirely refronted in the nineteenth century, combining Classical tripartite openings with Gothic battlements to produce a somewhat eclectic visual effect.

BALLYMONEY HOUSE
Ballymoney,
Kilbride
(c. 1710 and c. 1800)

Classical elements, including a tripartite Wyatt-style window and a lunette opening to the top floor, diminish in scale on each level, forming a graceful tiered quality in the façade. Originally built in the early eighteenth century, the house was greatly extended in the early nineteenth century.

Clonmannen Old Mansion.

(fig. 7)
**CLONMANNAN
HOUSE (OLD)**
Clonmannan
(c. 1700)

This drawing of 1819
shows the old house
at Clonmannan in its
original symmetrical form.
The breakfront, with its
pilasters, pediment and
oval window, show a
certain pretension on the
part of the original owner.
However, the effect is
negated somewhat by the
small proportions of the
building.

*Courtesy of the Irish
Architectural Archive.*

(fig. 8)
**CLONMANNAN
HOUSE (OLD)**
Clonmannan

Truncated in the early
twentieth century, much
of the early fabric remains
intact, including small-
pane sash windows which
contribute significantly to
the historic character of
the site.

The Williamite settlement created an atmosphere of security and confidence amongst the now overwhelmingly Protestant landed classes, which in time allowed building to take place on a wider scale, leading to the establishment of a significant number of new houses in the space of a generation following the Treaty of Limerick (1691). Many landowners, although keen to express their growing confidence and gentility, were constrained by a lack of resources in what was a kingdom recovering from decades of instability. Consequently, the first generation mansions of the late seventeenth and early eighteenth centuries were of relatively modest scale and plain appearance. Most were built with their owners or local builders acting as architects. These individuals stuck to well worn designs they had seen employed by their neighbours or in pattern books. The old house at Clonmannon (c. 1700), near Ashford, is a good case in point; a remarkably small, almost miniature, red brick residence built in a Classical style reminiscent of an Inigo Jones (1573–1652) design of the mid 1600s *(figs. 7-8)*. The now ruinous Tober House (c. 1720), near Dunlavin, was originally a rather modest two-storey over basement building with five narrow window openings to each floor and a simple shouldered doorcase *(fig. 9)*. Hillbrook House (c. 1725), near Carnew, which has now been demolished, was of comparable proportions and an even plainer appearance. Kilmacurragh House (1697), east of Rathdrum, built by Thomas Acton (fl. c. 1670–c. 1750) as a relatively straightforward compact residence of five bays and two storeys, is a notable exception and shows some well executed Classical pretensions, possibly the work of the Surveyor General Sir William Robinson (1645–1712) *(fig. 10)*.

(fig. 10)
KILMACURRAGH HOUSE
Westaston Demesne
(1697)

Kilmacurragh is believed to be the work of William Robinson (1645-1712), the Surveyor General from 1672 to 1700, whose work includes the Royal Hospital at Kilmainham, and Marshe's Library, both in nearby Dublin. The single-storey wings were added to the house in 1843 and the building was gutted by fire in 1976.

(fig. 9)
TOBER HOUSE
Tober Demesne,
Dunlavin
(c. 1720)

Although the door surround shows an awareness of the fashions of the time, the lack of symmetry to the ground floor fenestration shows that Tober, like many other gentry houses of the period, was probably the work of the owner and/or a builder.

(fig. 11)
SAUNDERSGROVE
HOUSE
Saundersgrove,
Stratford
(1716 and c. 1925)

The doorcase at
Saundersgrove is based
on models popularised by
James Gibbs (1682-1754)
through his publications
such as *The Book of
Architecture* (1728) and
*Rules for Drawing the
Several Parts of
Architecture* (1732).
Gibbs, a Scotsman who
studied in Rome, was one
of the earliest architects
in the British Isles to
disseminate his ideas
through books and his
designs remained popular
for much of the
eighteenth century.

The Hannoverian succession of George I (1660-1727) in 1714 and the frequently overlooked failure of the Jacobite Rising in Scotland the following year marked important stages in the growing sense of security of the Irish aristocracy and gentry. This in its turn engendered greater prosperity allowing, amongst other things, landowners to charge higher rents. All of this bolstered confidence, and a greater access to wealth helped foster a shift towards larger, more fashionable, and eventually more ostentatious buildings, and the more widespread use of architects to apply the latest styles. The now demolished original house at Saundersgrove, south east of Baltinglass, built in 1716 by Morley Saunders, clearly demonstrated the beginnings of this shift. The house was an impressive nine-bay three-storey block with basement, two fronts, and a tall parapet topped with urns and eagles. It was set in a garden with a formal canal and approached by a drive fronted with an impressive gate screen

with ball finials. The property was destroyed by fire in 1923, and most of the garden ornamentation is now gone, but what is believed to be the original granite doorcase, with heavily rusticated blocks in the manner of James Gibbs, (1682-1754) fronts the neo-Queen Anne dwelling (1925) built on the site *(fig. 11)*. Rosanna (c. 1720), near Ashford, although smaller than Saundersgrove and altered in later years, is a similarly well proportioned three-storey residence which demonstrates a confident red brick solidity *(fig. 12)*. The same can be said of Clermont (1730), Rathnew, built for Abraham Yarner, probably to designs by Francis Bindon (c. 1698–1765) of Dublin *(figs. 13-15)*. Here, however, the brick façade has been given greater interest with the inclusion of a more elaborate doorcase with flanking double Doric three-quarter columns, a first floor window encased with Ionic columns and a pediment, and, at second floor level, a lunette.

(fig. 12)
ROSANNA HOUSE
Rossanna Upper,
Ashford
(c. 1720)

By the 1720s, brick was
becoming increasingly
popular as a building
material for country houses throughout Ireland. It
was cheaper than stone
and proved particularly
suitable for the more
modest Palladian mansions. Rosanna House is
constructed in Flemish
bond, where the bricks
are laid so that alternate
headers and stretchers
appear in each course.

(fig. 13)
CLERMONT HOUSE
Newrath,
Rathnew
(1730)

Clermont is in many respects the archetypal early eighteenth-century Palladian country house. However, the symmetry and lines of the original composition were upset (c. 1900) when the single- and two-storey wings were added. The building became a school (c. 1950) upon which a large neo-Georgian extension was added to the south side.

(fig. 14)
CLERMONT HOUSE
Newrath,
Rathnew

Despite the changes to the exterior, much of Clermont's original interior detailing has survived, including the staircase, and much fielded panelling. The latter is a common feature of most early eighteenth-century houses in both town and country.

(fig. 15)
CLERMONT HOUSE
Newrath,
Rathnew

This photo of c. 1900 shows Clermont in its original form, before the addition of the wings.

Courtesy of the Irish Architectural Archive.

(fig. 16)
POWERSCOURT HOUSE
Powerscourt Demesne,
Enniskerry
(1731-40)

One of the finest country
houses in Ireland, Richard
Castle's (1690-1751)
Powerscourt employed a
fashionable Palladian-style
arrangement whereby the
central residential block
was linked to services
pavilion blocks by curved
or lateral wings or screen
walls.

(fig. 17)
POWERSCOURT HOUSE
Powerscourt Demesne,
Enniskerry

Many of Castle's compositions
involved the application of
Baroque details in what were
otherwise Palladian forms, as
the parapet over the pediment at Powerscourt House
shows.

(fig. 18)
POWERSCOURT HOUSE
Powerscourt Demesne,
Enniskerry

An elaborate iron gate
enhances the ornamental
quality of the grounds at
Powerscourt and includes
a trompe l'oeil central
panel depicting the per-
spective view down a
pathway.

(fig. 19)
POWERSCOURT HOUSE
Powerscourt Demesne,
Enniskerry

Originally developed as
an integral component
of the house by Castle,
the terraced gardens
were improved by the
Scottish-born Daniel
Robertson (fl. 1812-49)
in the 1840s. Influenced
by the gardens at the
Villa Butera (now the Villa
Trabia) in Sicily, according
to the Viscount's memoirs
Robertson supervised
much of the execution
of the gardens from
the comfort of a
wheelbarrow!

Houses such as Clermont, Saundersgrove, and Rossana, with their emphasis on symmetry, regularity of fenestration, and Classical detailing, all show to some degree the influence of Palladianism. This style, which espoused the ideals of the sixteenth-century Italian architect Andrea Palladio (1508–80), was popularised throughout these islands by a fashionable circle led by Lord Burlington (1694–1753), and architects Colen Campbell (d. 1729) and William Kent (1685–1748). It was to dominate architecture in both Ireland and Britain in the half century after 1714. County Wicklow possesses two of the finest examples of large Palladian mansions to be seen anywhere in either country: Powerscourt House (1731–40) *(figs. 16-19)* and Russborough House (1741–48) *(figs. 20-27)*. Both buildings were designed by

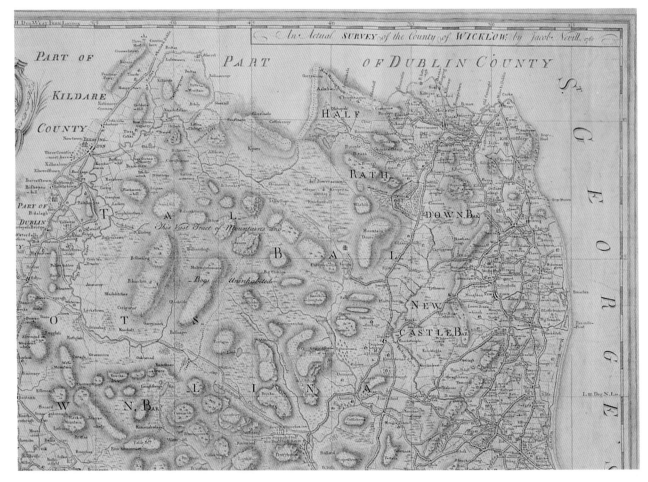

**COUNTY WICKLOW
(1760)**

A mid eighteenth-century topographical map by Jacob Nevill shows the extent of country houses County Wicklow possessed by 1760. Many more would be built in the following decades.

Courtesy of the National Library of Ireland.

the German born architect, Richard Cassells (1690–1751), who was known in Ireland as Richard Castle. Powerscourt, in the north east of the county near Enniskerry, was granted to Sir Richard Wingfield (b. pre-1550) in 1603. In 1731 his descendant, another Sir Richard Wingfield (1706-51), afterwards 1st Viscount Powerscourt, commissioned Castle to build a new larger dwelling around his existing residence, which itself had evolved from a medieval tower house. Over the next nine years Castle created a sumptuous granite mansion in a typically Palladian manner. The three-storey central block with five-bay pedimented breakfront is flanked by single storey links to two-storey wings with quadrant walls beyond, each including a pedimented Doric archway, and terminating in an obelisk topped with the Wingfield crest. Internally, the ground floor rooms had coffered ceilings decorated with sea shells in stucco, and there was a grand colonnaded saloon. The symmetry of the original composition was broken in 1787 when the garden front was raised to three storeys. The interior of the main central section was completely gutted by a fire in 1974, but the grandeur of Powerscourt, set against the dramatic backdrop of the Sugar Loaf Mountain, remains largely undiminished.

(fig. 20)
RUSSBOROUGH HOUSE
Russborough
(1741-52)

Richard Castle's (1690-1751) collaborator at Russborough, Francis Bindon (c. 1698-1765) was a County Clare-born architect who also worked under Sir Edward Lovett Pearce (c. 1699-1733) in the early 1730s. It is likely that Bindon completed the unfinished work at Russborough after Castle's death in 1751.

(fig. 21)
RUSSBOROUGH HOUSE
Russborough

Russborough House is constructed in granite mined at nearby Golden Hill, and is enlivened with urns, swags and heraldic beasts, with Classical figures set in niches within the colonnades.

(fig. 22)
**JOSEPH LEESON
afterwards 1st Earl of
Milltown by Pompeo
Batoni
(1708-87)**

Joseph Leeson (1701-83)
inherited his father's for-
tune in 1741 and in the
same year purchased the
lands which were to
become the Russborough
estate. He was elected an
MP in 1743. A lover of all
things Italian, he visited
Rome in 1744 and 1751,
collecting large amounts of
Roman artefacts for his
new home. Leeson was
created Earl of Milltown in
1756. His descendants
remained in possession of
the house until 1932.

© *Courtesy of the National
Gallery of Ireland.*

(fig. 23)
**RUSSBOROUGH HOUSE
Russborough**

The Francini (or
LaFrancini) brothers were
Swiss-born stuccodores
who settled in Ireland and
created some of the finest
interior decoration in the
country. Apart from
Russborough, they were
also responsible the
stucco-work at Castletown
House, Carton House,
both in County Kildare,
Riverstown House, County
Cork, and Curraghmore,
County Waterford.

*Courtesy of the Irish
Architechural Archive.*

(fig. 24)
**RUSSBOROUGH HOUSE
Russborough**

A view of the sweep
to the entrance that,
together with the curved
colonnades, represents
the most direct form of
ornamentation on the
exterior of the house.

(fig. 27)
RUSSBOROUGH HOUSE
Russborough
(c. 1745)

The design of the gate
way to Russborough is
based on a triumphal
arch: freestanding monu-
mental gateways which
originated in Rome in
the second century BC.

(fig. 25)
RUSSBOROUGH HOUSE
Russborough

The use of the Classical
order on the elevations
of the pavilion blocks,
including an engaged
central frontispiece, pro-
duces a graceful grandeur
that belies the utilitarian
nature of the services
carried out within.

(fig. 26)
RUSSBOROUGH HOUSE
Russborough

Locally-sourced granite
has proven extremely
durable and retains the
crisp intricacy of finely
carved detailing, including
the foliate motifs and
Composite capitals
illustrated.

Castle, in collaboration with Francis Bindon (c. 1698-1765), the architect responsible for Clermont, commenced work on Russborough House shortly after the completion of Powerscourt in 1740 *(figs. 25-26)*. His commission had come from Joseph Leeson, 1st Earl of Milltown (1701-83), the son of a wealthy Dublin brewer. With Russborough, unlike Powerscourt, Castle did not have to contend with an existing structure. It is probably for this reason that Russborough is generally regarded as a more satisfactory building, described by Mark Bence-Jones as 'arguably the most beautiful house in Ireland'. The classic Palladian format was employed again but, in this case, two storeys over a tall basement cen-

tral block were linked to two-storey wings with outer walls that disguised the outbuildings. The wings sit in front of the line of the main block, linked to it by gracefully curving Doric colonnades. The overall front elevation, stretching a grandiose 215 metres including the flanking walls, is much longer than Powerscourt. This lengthy frontage is approached side on from a long drive entered through an impressive triumphal arch (c. 1745), a miniature Palladian masterpiece in its own right *(fig. 27)*. The full splendour of the composition gradually reveals itself to the visitor. The interior, which like the exterior has escaped any later alterations, contains principal rooms decorated with Baroque plasterwork believed to be by the renowned

(fig. 28)
SHELTON ABBEY
Shelton Abbey, Arklow
(1770 and 1819)

A relatively plain late eighteenth-century pile built by Ralph Howard (1740-89), the house was reconceived as an elaborate Gothic fantasy in the early nineteenth century to designs by Sir Richard Morrison (1767-1844). Delicate plasterwork ceilings enrich the interior spaces of the composition.

(fig. 29)
SHELTON ABBEY
Shelton Abbey,
Arklow

Supplementing the innumerable gables, finials, pinnacles and chimney stacks, a slender turret forms a focal point of the highly enriched roofline at Shelton Abbey.

Francini brothers Paulo (1695–1770) and Filippo (1702-79). Marble fireplaces also survive, as does the wonderfully ebullient Rococo plasterwork around the main staircase. At both Powerscourt and Russborough, it has been suggested that Richard Castle also landscaped the original grounds along the then fashionable geometric lines, the work at the latter costing in excess of £30,000 – a massive sum at the time. Though relatively few landowners in Wicklow, or anywhere else in Ireland, could aspire to the exuberant grandeur of a Powerscourt or a Russborough, by the middle of the eighteenth century many were affluent enough to make important architectural statements in their own right. One such was the Dublin banker, David La Touche, who expended £30,000 in the mid 1750s on the construc-

tion of a large new house, Bellevue, at Delgany. Another, Ralph Howard MP (1740-89), afterwards 1st Viscount Wicklow, built the even larger eleven-bay two-storcy mansion of Shelton (1770 and 1819), near Arklow *(figs. 28-29)*. Lower down the pecking order, the county gentry also began to express their status with a spate of new houses. The former home of the Chamney family, Ballyraheen House (c. 1760), north of Shillelagh, is a five-bay two-storey building with a full height canted projection and pedimented doorcase *(fig. 30)*. The flanking walls, once again disguising the farm buildings, are an interesting example of how, by the 1750s and 1760s, the tenets of Palladianism had filtered through to relatively small scale compositions.

(fig. 30)
BALLYRAHEEN HOUSE
Ballyraheen Crossroads,
Ballyraheen
(c. 1760)

Ballyraheen was the site of a battle during the 1798 Rebellion, and the façade of the house still bares the marks of musket shot. The then owner of the house, Colonel Chamney, was killed in the fighting.

(fig. 31)
AVONDALE HOUSE
Avondale
(1779)

Avondale may have been designed by James Wyatt (1746-1813), one of the most prolific English architects of the second half on the eighteenth century. It is now widely known as the former home of the politician, Charles Stewart Parnell (1846-91), whose ancestor, Sir John Parnell (1744-1801), inherited the estate in 1795 from his cousin, Samuel Hayes.

(fig. 32)
AVONDALE HOUSE
Avondale

Finely carved bas relief panels incorporating Classical motifs punctuate the breakfront at Avondale. A cut-stone plaque records the historic associations with Charles Stuart Parnell.

(fig. 33)
AVONDALE HOUSE
Avondale

A portrait by Sydney P. Hall of the Irish National leader Charles Stuart Parnell (1846-91) who remains the most celebrated occupant of Avondale.

© *and courtesy of the National Gallery of Ireland.*

(fig. 34)
MOUNT KENNEDY
Mount Kennedy Demesne,
Newtown
Mountkennedy
(1782-84)

Diocletian windows, such
as to the centre of the first
floor, first appeared in the
thermae (baths) of Diocletian,
Rome, in the early fourth
century. They were revived
by Palladio in the sixteenth
century and became a com-
monly used form in both
Palladian and neo-Classical
compositions throughout the
Georgian period.

*Courtesy of the Irish
Architectural Archive.*

The building of new country houses, as well as the remodelling of older ones along more fashionable lines, was to increase in the latter decades of the eighteenth century, particularly in the boom years of Irish legislative independence (1782–1800). The resulting houses witnessed the shift from the Palladian style to the slightly more rigid and impersonal, but nonetheless graceful, neo-Classicism, as popularised by the Scottish architect Robert Adam (1728–92). The change in style can be seen clearly in Avondale (1779), near Rathdrum, built for Samuel Hayes MP *(figs. 31-33)*. The overall composition is simple and rather austere, with a square plan and a front elevation enlivened only by a simple pedimented bay and portico. At Clonmannon, the new larger house (c. 1780) that superseded the brick built dwelling (c. 1700) is of a blocklike appearance similar to Avondale. Only the pedimented entrance breaks the sparse lines of the front façade. Mount Kennedy, built in 1782–84 to designs attributed to Thomas Cooley (1740–84), is remarkably like Clonmannon although, with a Diocletian window directly above the doorway *(fig. 34)*, marginally more interesting. The simple forms of the neo-Classical idiom proved particularly easy to apply to the smaller houses that the county's minor gentry and strong farmers continued to build in numbers. Oldfort and Lodge *(fig. 35)* (both c. 1780), Newcastle, both show the influence of the style in the pared down and somewhat rustic form that was to prove popular throughout Ireland well into the middle of the next century. Despite the trend towards neo-Classicism in the late 1700s, the more exuberant Palladian interpretation of Classical architecture, which had arguably proved more popular in Ireland than it had in Britain, did not lose favour completely as Charleville (1797), built by Whitmore Davis for 1st Viscount Monck (1769-1802), illustrates *(figs. 36-37)*.

(fig. 35)
LODGE
Newcastle Upper,
Newcastle
(c. 1780)

The smaller country houses of the late eighteenth century maintained the clean lines of their larger counterparts, but frequently dispensed with costly overt neo-Classical detailing. Lodge is very similar to its near, and probably contemporary, neighbour Oldfort. Here, decoration has been restricted to the fanlight.

(fig. 36)
CHARLEVILLE HOUSE
Charleville Demesne,
Enniskerry
(1797)

Charleville House remains
one of the most memo-
rable country houses in
County Wicklow, and
features a distinctive
Classically ordered breakfront. It was undoubtedly
inspired by the very
similar Lucan House,
County Dublin, designed
c. 1775 by Sir William
Chambers (1723-96).

(fig. 37)
CHARLEVILLE HOUSE
Charleville Demesne,
Enniskerry

The entrance at
Charleville House incor-
porates some finely exe-
cuted detailing, including
this composite capital
and reeded frieze with
rosette motif.

Private country houses were not the only means through which Wicklow's aristocracy and gentry found architectural expression. They also accomplished this, and at the same time furthered their commercial interests, by establishing and developing estate villages. The late seventeenth-century development of Blessington by Archbishop Boyle is a good early example; the linear form of the settlement is based, appropriately enough given that the landlord was such an important cleric, around the focal point of the church. Dunlavin, the creation of the Tynte family of Tynte Park, was also given a linear layout with the market house (1743) as its centrepiece *(fig. 38)*. This striking cruciform Palladian-style building with corner colonnades and a fluted stone dome was probably built to a design by the prolific Richard Castle. It is relatively small in scale, but through its prominent situation in the village's main street and its sheer bravado, it succeeds in dominating the entire scene. At Stratford on Slaney (1780s), established by Edward Augustus Stratford (c. 1741-1801) the 2nd Earl of Aldborough, it is the neat symmetrical layout of the village itself, rather than any particular building, that impresses *(figs. 39-40)*.

(fig. 38)
DUNLAVIN
MARKET HOUSE
Market Square/Main
Street/Killcullen Street,
Dunlavin
(1743)

The market house at Dunlavin is one of the finest provincial eighteenth-century public buildings in the whole country, and has been described by architectural historian Dr. Maurice Craig as, 'The apogee of the small court or market house as the centrepiece of a formal square...'.

(fig. 39)
DUBLIN STREET
Stratford
(c. 1840)

Although now a reasonably quiet and unassuming village, Stratford contains a number of relatively substantial houses which give some indication of its past importance.

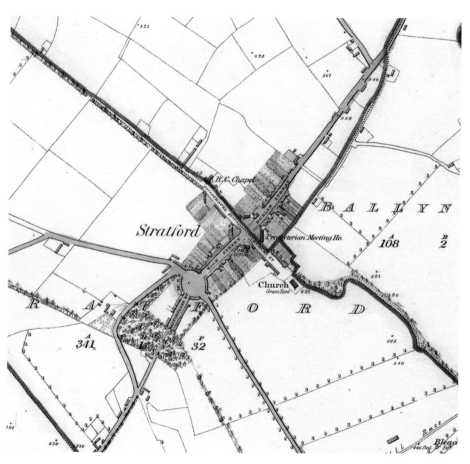

(fig. 40)
SECTION OF ORDNANCE SURVEY MAP OF WICKLOW 1:10,560 SHEET 21 (surveyed 1838, published 1839)

Stratford on Slaney was established as a model village based around the local textile industry. It was partly settled and developed by workers from Paisley in Scotland. At its height it had housing for over 1,000 workers, churches for Church of Ireland, Presbyterian and Roman Catholic denominations, a benefit society, and a library.

Courtesy of Trinity College Dublin.

As well as furthering their own interests and those of their tenantry through what were essentially private building works, Wicklow's landed classes, sitting as the County Grand Jury, were also responsible for overseeing the construction of public and administrative projects such as roads, bridges, prisons and courthouses. One of the oldest and largest buildings that the Grand Jury was responsible for, the County Gaol in Wicklow Town (originally 1702), is a suitably austere rubble stone edifice and one of the best surviving examples of its type in the whole country *(fig. 41)*. Clara Bridge (c. 1680) is a remarkably well preserved

six-arch structure of even greater vintage *(fig. 42)*. The narrow bridge is less than 3.25 metres wide and is particularly striking to twenty-first century motorists. Length rather than width distinguishes the nineteen-arch Arklow Bridge *(fig. 43)* (c. 1754–56) which, built to a design by Andrew Noble, is the longest multiple-arch bridge in Ireland. Although the bridge was widened in 1959 to cope with increasing traffic levels, the downstream side remains close to its original form. In spite of such road widening throughout the county during the twentieth century, some Georgian Grand Jury road furniture has sur-

(fig. 41)
WICKLOW GAOL
Kilmantin Hill,
Wicklow
(originally 1702)

Although there has been a gaol on this site since 1702, much of the present complex dates from rebuilds of the late 1790s, 1820s and 1840s. Much of the work carried out in the late 1790s was due directly to the pressure put on the old building by the increased number of prisoners, mainly United Irishmen.

(fig. 42)
CLARA BRIDGE
Ballyhad Upper/
Clarabeg South,
Clara
(c. 1680)

Clara Bridge is undoubt-
edly amongst the most
noteworthy bridges in
County Wicklow, not only
because of its great age,
but also because of its
picturesque setting in the
beautiful Vale of Clara.

(fig. 43)
ARKLOW BRIDGE
Arklow
(c. 1754-56 and 1959)

Locally known as
'The Nineteen Arches',
Arklow Bridge's sheer
length makes it one of
the most striking sites
in the town.

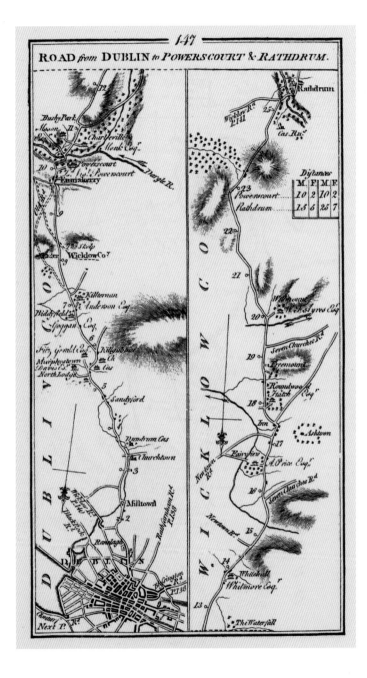

vived, including at least four triangular granite milestones (c. 1760) along what is now the N81 south of the Hollywood crossroads *(fig. 44)*. A more unusual milestone of similar vintage survives set into the wall next to the main gateway to the grounds of Kilranelagh House (c. 1780), east of Baltinglass, with charmingly naïve hand symbols pointing the way to the major towns and villages *(fig. 45)*. Another remarkable eighteenth-century survivor, the Upper Wicklow Head lighthouse (1778–81), was the work of the Revenue Commissioners rather than the County Grand Jury. Designed by engineer John Trail (d. 1801), this six-stage tapering octagonal tower was originally one of a pair; the similar lower tower was replaced (1818) *(figs. 46-47)*. With its cut stone finish and dressed granite quoins and window surrounds, the structure has been described as 'the most grandiose of lighthouses in the British Isles'. The building was refitted in 1836, having been gutted by fire, while a brick dome was added in 1866.

**TAYLOR AND
SKINNER MAP
(1777)**

The relative improvement in roads in the late eighteenth century led to the publication of an increasing number of maps and travellers' guides. *The Taylor and Skinner Guide*, which shows sections of roads in south west Wicklow, also marks the positions of some churches and the major country houses; the homes of the county's richest inhabitants were of as great an interest to the eighteenth-century traveller as they are today.

Courtesy of the National Library of Ireland.

(fig. 44)
HOLLYWOOD CROSSROADS
Hollywood
(c. 1760)

The triangular inscribed stone form was used for Grand Jury milestones throughout the country during this period. However, in the first half of the nineteenth century cast-iron varieties began to appear.

(fig. 45)
KILRANELAGH HOUSE
Kilranelagh
(c. 1780)

This 'milestone', embedded in the demesne wall at Kinranelagh House, faces out on to the intersection of two roads, hence the long list of destinations.

(fig. 46)
UPPER WICKLOW HEAD LIGHTHOUSES
Dunbur Head
(1778-81 and 1818)

For many centuries the rocky coastline of County Wicklow was a particular hazard to shipping, and necessitated the erection of the Wicklow Head lighthouses by the Revenue Commissioners in an attempt to eradicate some of the danger. Two towers were needed in order to distinguish between Wicklow Head and Hook Head in County Wexford.

(fig. 47)
UPPER WICKLOW HEAD LIGHTHOUSE
Dunbur Head
(1778-81)

An elegantly-profiled, tapering octagonal shaft, finely dressed in the Classical style, forms a dramatic focal point on the rocky coastal landscape.

The most common type of eighteenth-century public building was the church. As previously noted, many of Wicklow's medieval churches, in common with those in other counties, suffered damage in the religious upheavals of the sixteenth century. Given the unsettled conditions of the following century, the still embattled Church of Ireland remained to a large extent restricted in its efforts at renewal or rebuilding. Saint Paul's Church (1609), Bray, believed to have been built on the site of an earlier building, is exceptional. In the relatively peaceful late 1600s two new churches were built at Blessington and Hollywood.

Both these buildings are interesting, not only because they are rare seventeenth-century survivors, but also because they differ from each other in terms of style and scale. Saint Kevin's Church (c. 1680–90), Hollywood, harks back to Early Christian Irish churches *(fig. 48)*. It is a small rectangular gable-ended building perched on a hill, with battered walls finished in lime plaster over slate, a barrel vaulted roof, pronounced stone parapets, and a simple bellcote. Saint Mary's Church (1681), Blessington, is a much larger affair which in its original form followed the later medieval pattern of nave and tower *(fig. 49)*.

(fig. 48)
SAINT KEVIN'S CHURCH
Knockroe,
Hollywood
(c. 1680-90)

Although new churches were built in greater numbers in the late seventeenth century, many rural buildings, such as Saint Kevin's, were simple small-scale structures, little different from their medieval counterparts.

(fig. 49)
SAINT MARY'S CHURCH
Market Square,
Blessington
(1681)

The richer landlords could invest in larger, more impressive churches. Blessington was originally the property of Michael Boyle (1609-1702), who by the late 1670s had become Lord High Chancellor of Ireland and Archbishop of Armagh. Saint Mary's Church, which when built stood opposite the gates to Boyle's impressive Blessington House, reflects its builder's elevated status.

(fig. 50)
**CHRIST CHURCH
Delgany
(1789)**

Christ Church was built by Whitmore Davis for Peter La Touche (d. 1830) who is commemorated by a large monument on the east wall of the nave, erected by his son David. Such is the scale of the monument that the rector promptly reordered the altar to the north wall!

(fig. 51)
**SAINT SAVIOUR'S
CHURCH
Main Street,
Rathdrum
(1796 and part
rebuilt 1837-8)**

By the late eighteenth century, 'gothick' detailing was beginning to permeate church architecture, as the doorway and windows on this church show.

**SAINT LIVINIUS'
CHURCH
Church Hill,
Wicklow
(1777)**

A plain Church of Ireland church conforming to a form and arrangement advocated by the Board of First Fruits (fl. c. 1711-1833). A sturdy entrance tower, stepping in at each stage, identifies the building in the townscape.

SAINT LIVINIUS'
CHURCH
Church Hill,
Wicklow

Iron work railings and a
fanlight-style overpanel
enhance the design quali-
ty of the composition.

SAINT LIVINIUS'
CHURCH
Church Hill,
Wicklow

Delicate stained glass
panels lend a jewel-like
quality to the interior.

SAINT LIVINIUS'
CHURCH
Church Hill,
Wicklow

The nave of the church
incorporates a wealth
of important joinery
including carved pews,
an increasingly-rare U-plan
gallery, a pipe organ,
and an exposed roof
construction with distinctive fan-style panels.

In the more tranquil climes after the ending of the Williamite Wars and the passing of
the Penal Laws in 1704–06, the now more
assertive Church of Ireland began a more struc-
tured programme of building. To assist in this,
church authorities set up the Board of First
Fruits in 1711 (flourished until 1833). The role
of this body was to gather a building fund out
of which the cost of new construction, usually footed by the larger landowners, could be
supported. Saint Michael's Church (1716),
Aghold, an early example of these efforts, is
also noteworthy in that it follows a T-plan
more common to Presbyterian and Roman
Catholic buildings. Most of the Established
Church's extant efforts date from after 1777. In
the face of the stiffer competition that came
with the easing of the Penal Laws, members of
the Church of Ireland, of which there were relatively high numbers in County Wicklow,
embarked on a more determined campaign of
building. The church at Delgany (1789), built
solely at the expense of Peter La Touche
(d.1830) to a design by Whitmore Davis, is an
example of the zeal of a single local landlord
(*fig. 50*). In comparison the building of the
new church at Rathdrum (1796) was to a large
extent achieved through the enthusiasm of a
number of parishioners, who contributed
£1,000 towards the cost (*fig. 51*). Both these
churches follow the nave and tower form mentioned above, although the tower at Delgany
rises from the roof of the nave rather than
standing in front of it, whilst the tower at
Rathdrum is flanked by large side porches.

(fig. 52)
BOLAND'S
22 Main Street,
Arklow
(c. 1760)

The growing prosperity
of the urban middle and
professional classes by the
middle of the eighteenth
century led to an increase
in large town houses in
Arklow and Wicklow. This
example is particularly
substantial and compares
favourably with contem-
porary town houses in
Dublin.

(fig. 53)
BOLAND'S
22 Main Street,
Arklow

A cut-stone Gibbsian or
block-and-start doorcase
contributes to the
Classical theme of the
composition.

NEWTOWN
MOUNTKENNEDY
(c. 1800)

A middle-size house
incorporating balanced
proportions on a symmet-
rical façade introduces a
formal element in the
street scene of Newtown
Mountkennedy.

NEWTOWN
MOUNTKENNEDY

An Ionic doorcase and
'cobweb' fanlight
enhance the elegant,
uncluttered quality of
the design.

(fig. 54)
ACE FLOORING
Main Street,
Blessington
(c. 1790)

By the close of the 1700s
Classical detailing was to
be found even in the mod-
est town houses of smaller
centres such as Blessington.
Local builders would have
had ready access to such
designs through widely
available pattern books.

The impact of wealthy landed gentlemen, such as Peter La Touche, on eighteenth-century Wicklow is quite clear; but the relative prosperity of the county meant that those lower down the social order could make their own modest mark on the landscape. This was particularly so in the towns. The rising merchant and professional classes included many Roman Catholics who, excluded from the purchase of land, turned to trade, and wished their homes to reflect their increasing wealth. Number 22 Main Street, Arklow (c. 1760), is one of the county's finest mid-Georgian town houses *(figs. 52-53)*; a large five-bay three-storey brick built terraced dwelling with a Gibbs-influenced painted stone doorcase and moulded architraves to the ground floor windows. A large Edwardian shopfront has upset the composition but the façade maintains an air of dignified self assurance. Similar confidence on a smaller two-storey scale is found at Blessington, where several of the terraced properties fronting onto the main street (c. 1780), now largely converted to shops, have similar sub-Gibbsian doorcases in granite with decorative fanlights *(fig. 54)*. Such fanlights were in many respects the countrywide trademark of Georgian merchant class aspirations.

(fig. 56)
**HUNTER'S HOUSE
HOTEL
Ballinapark,
Ashford**

A detail of the early
fittings to the openings
which contribute to
the historic quality of
the site.

(fig. 55)
**HUNTER'S HOUSE
HOTEL
Ballinapark,
Ashford
(c. 1720)**

Tucked in at the side
of a now quiet road near
Ashford, Hunter's House
Hotel is one of County
Wicklow's hidden gems
and still retains the air of
an early eighteenth-century coaching inn. The front
façade was probably
altered c. 1820, around
the time when coaching
throughout Ireland was
reaching its peak.

Set within a rural rather than an urban con-
text, Hunter's House Hotel (c. 1720), Ashford,
is not only one of Wicklow's most outstanding
buildings belonging to the ranks of the commercial middle classes, but an extremely rare
and remarkably intact example of an early
eighteenth-century coaching inn, complete
with stable yard *(figs. 55-56)*. The inn was built
to serve the busy route between Dublin and
Wicklow. Although the front façade, with tripartite windows and an entrance having an
elliptical fanlight and sidelights, gives the
building a late Georgian appearance, it is probably much earlier. A relatively steeply pitched
double pile roof, a low ceiling interior with
exposed roughly hewn oak beams, an oak staircase, and at least one fireplace with 'eared' surround, all suggest a building of around 1720.

DOWNSHIRE HOTEL
Main Street,
Blessington
(c. 1820)

This well-composed, substantial house has been successfully converted to a commercial use without adversely affecting the historic character of the site. A cut-stone portico embellishes the composition, and enhances the appeal of the site in the streetscape.

(fig. 57)
DELGANY
Killincarrig
(pre-1700)

Once a common feature of both urban and rural areas in Wicklow, comparatively few thatched cottages have survived into the twenty-first century, particularly along the traditionally more prosperous eastern edge of the county. The cottage pictured remains an important early exponent of the genre, and includes features characteristic of rubble stone ranges, including stout supporting buttresses.

MOYNE
(c. 1820)

Subtle features such as early or original timber sash windows enhance the visual appeal of a site, but are always under threat of replacement with modern articles that can be detrimental to the character of an historic building.

(fig. 58)
DWYER-McALLISTER
COTTAGE
Derrynamuck
(c. 1780)

This cottage was the scene of a famous skirmish during 1799, when Sam McAllister (d. 1799) drew the fire of government soldiers in order to allow his fellow United Irishmen to escape. McAllister and three others were killed, but the resourceful Michael Dwyer (1772-1825), a noted United Irish leader in the area, escaped and hid out in the Wicklow mountains, evading capture for another four years. The building is now a National Monument and the single bay portion to the north end was reconstructed in 1992.

Most of the population of eighteenth-century Wicklow lived in the countryside, working the land belonging to the large estates. Their means were limited and consequently their houses were generally small and lacking in any architectural pretension. These vernacular dwellings, one room deep, single-storey and rectangular in form, were built in stone extracted from surrounding fields together with wood and thatch gathered locally. When family size dictated and resources permitted, such dwellings would be extended lengthways, or the walls raised and a loft level or second floor added. A comparatively rare surviving example of the vernacular form in County Wicklow can be seen on the road between Delgany and Killincarrig (pre–1700) with characteristic low proportions, whitewashed stone walls, and a loft level in the steeply pitched hipped thatched roof *(fig. 57)*. In common with many such properties, the fenestration has been altered at some point; the original openings were probably much smaller and possibly orig-

inally unglazed. The large buttresses are also a later feature. This particular house is of the 'hearth and lobby' type where the hearth and the entrance are in line with each other at the centre of the building, a form that is more common in the arable areas in the east of the country. The Dwyer-McAllister cottage (c. 1780) at Derrynamuck, near the Glen of Imaal, is an example of an alternative type, the 'direct entry' or 'long house' *(fig. 58)*. The hearth is placed against what was originally an end gable. This type is more common to pastoral upland areas of the north and west of the country where both people and animals frequently lived under the one roof and clear access was needed for entry of livestock. County Wicklow is something of an anomaly in eastern Ireland in that it contains a number of this type of vernacular dwelling; it may have something to do with the contrasting landscape of the county, but the phenomenon has never been fully explained.

DONARD
(c. 1780)

A very well preserved example of a typical modest-scale and sparsely-detailed gentleman's residence.

DONARD

A simple flat iron gate incorporates an elegantly turned handle attesting to the craft of the local iron monger or smithy.

The Nineteenth Century

Over a century of relative peace and tranquillity was shattered by the Rebellion of 1798. The United Irishmen, a movement inspired by the ideals of the French Revolution, attempted to forcibly cut Ireland's connection to Britain with the aid of an invasion force from republican France. The United Irishmen had a particularly strong following in south-east Leinster. In Wicklow they were able to muster at least 14,000 adherents by 1798 and when rebellion broke out in summer of that year the county witnessed bloody battles at Newtown Mountkennedy and Arklow. Following the defeat of the bulk of the Leinster insurgents in late June 1798, several thousand of the more militant rebels took to Wicklow's mountainous interior from where they launched guerrilla attacks upon the government forces. These attacks continued until late in the year when an amnesty by the military encouraged many to finally surrender, including the insurgent leader, General Joseph Holt (1756-1826). A small number of United Irishmen under the leadership of the resourceful Michael Dwyer (1772-1825) continued their resistance until the end of 1803. By this stage the government had plans that would ensure that the mountainous terrain of Wicklow, whose inaccessibility had been a haven for outlaws and rebels for centuries, would never pose a problem again. These plans centred on the creation of a 56 kilometre military road through the mountains from Rathfarnham in South Dublin County to Aughavannagh, making access much easier for both soldiers and heavy artillery; a strategy that had first been mooted by the Elizabethan administration in the 1580s. The road was to serve a similar pacifying purpose to the road cut through the Scottish Highlands in the wake of the Jacobite Rising of 1745. Appropriately, two hundred soldiers of the Highland Regiment were put to work on its construction in August 1800. The road itself, completed in 1809, is relatively unremarkable. The engineer, Captain Alexander Taylor, was instructed to follow the contours of the land rather than incur the expense of constructing bridges. More impressive are the five barracks built at various points, each a day's march apart, along its length: Glencree (1806); Laragh (1804), Glendalough; Drumgoff (after 1803), Glenmalure; Leitrim (before 1809), Glen of Imaal; and Aughavannagh (1803). Glencree survives as the only example retaining its original form, and remains a massive part three- and four-storey symmetrical building overlooking the glen, consisting of an eleven-bay central block flanked by two-bay gabled projections, with openings dressed in granite *(figs. 59-60)*. To the western side of this a large U-shaped two-storey range of ancillary buildings is built into the bank of the slope. The whole complex is a prominent feature for miles around.

MOYNE
(c. 1820)

A group of small-scale houses of some urban vernacular value presenting an appealing feature of rustic quality in the street scene.

(fig. 59)
GLENCREE BARRACKS
Aurora,
Glencree
(1806)

Following the final defeat of Napoleon in 1815 the Military Road and the barracks along it became obsolete. Glencree was gradually wound down as a barracks (records indicate each barrack was occupied by just one sergeant by 1822) and was used intermittently in the 1830s and 40s as a store, slowly falling into disrepair. In 1858 it was acquired by the Oblate Fathers who repaired the buildings and converted them to a Reformatory School. They also added a chapel to the site. Saint Kevin's Reformatory School

vacated Glencree in 1940 and a few years later the complex passed to the Minister of Supply. Between 1945 and 1950 it served a UN-sponsored refugee centre for German and Polish children. In 1974 the, by now derelict, buildings were leased to 'Working for Peace', a group concerned with establishing a refuge for people caught up in the violence in Northern Ireland. In the following years the group restored the buildings and established 'The Glencree Centre for Reconciliation', offering a range of courses and activities concerned with peace and non-violence. A new separate wing was added to the site in 1994.

(fig. 60)
GLENCREE BARRACKS
Aurora,
Glencree

Between each tier of window openings a cast-iron tie plate expresses on the exterior the means of fixing the beams that support the internal floors.

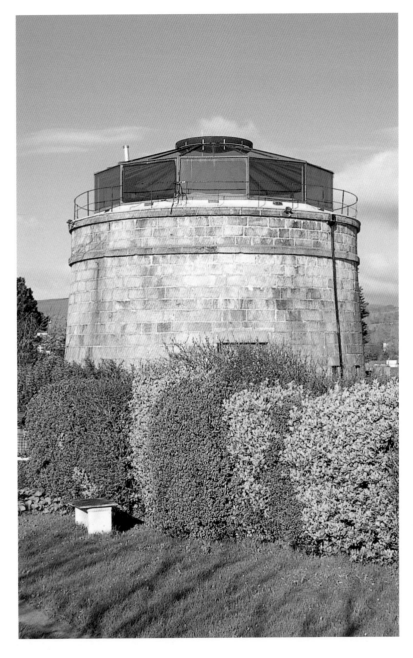

(fig. 61)
BRAY MARTELLO TOWER
Strand Road
Bray
(1804-5)

Irish Martello Towers were
built to a relatively uniform
design, with thick battered
walls of dressed granite,
two floors and an open
roof level.

Glencree's positioning meant that it had a
view of the coastline and any hostile French ves-
sels. Martello towers were the first line of security against such an invasion. These were a collection of generally uniform squat two-stage battered coastal watchtowers built by the government from 1804 onwards. A large number, for
obvious reasons, were concentrated around
Dublin. Bray, then little more than a large village but strategically important due to its relative closeness to the capital, witnessed the building of three Martello towers along its coastline.
Of these one survives (1804–5), set on the rise
to the north end of the present Strand Road and
now converted to residential use *(fig. 61)*. The
defeat of the 1798 United Irishmen and Robert
Emmet's (1778-1803) Rebellion of 1803, as well
as the defeat of the French navy at Trafalgar in
1805, meant that by the time the Military Road
was completed and the Martello tower chain
operational, the danger of invasion had largely
passed. With the final defeat of Napoleon in
1815 both gradually slipped into redundancy;
Glencree, for instance, was adapted as a store
and then a reformatory school. Overtly military
structures aside, the Napoleonic Wars had an
even greater indirect impact on Wicklow's built
landscape. The booming war time economy,
which lasted for years after hostilities had actu-
ally ceased, allowed many to plough their prof-
its into new building schemes.

(fig. 62)
BALLYCURRY HOUSE
Ballycurry Demesne,
Ashford
(1807 and c. 1875)

A substantial, Classical-style house built on the site of an earlier house for Charles Tottenham to the designs of Francis Johnson (1761-1829). A projecting wing was added in the late nineteenth century.

(fig. 64)
BALLYNURE HOUSE
Ballynure Demesne,
Grange Con

Deep surrounds to the gables are enriched by paired consoles, or modillions, and form a pediment-style motif that continues the Classical style theme of the house.

(fig. 63)
BALLYNURE HOUSE
Ballynure Demesne,
Grange Con
(c. 1800)

A large, symmetrically-planned house built for the Carroll family at the turn of the nineteenth century. Tripartite Wyatt-style window openings to the gabled end bays lend a graceful tone to the design.

49

(fig. 65)
CASTLE HOWARD
Castlehoward
(1811)

Built for Robert Howard (d. 1834?), Castle Howard represents one of the earliest attempts to produce an archaeologically-grounded Gothic pile, and forms a bridge between Gothicised Georgian compositions of a century earlier and the Gothic Revivalist movement inspired by the writings of John Ruskin (1819-1900) and Augustus Welby Northmore Pugin (1812-52).

(fig. 66)
CASTLE HOWARD
Castlehoward

Pointed-arch windows incorporating mullioned openings and decorative tracery contribute significantly to the medieval quality of Sir Richard Morrison's scheme.

The upper echelons of the landed classes, as always, proved the most enthusiastic builders. The early decades of the nineteenth century witnessed the construction of new country houses throughout a county whose closeness to the capital, despite Dublin's loss of prestige following the passage of the Act of Union (1800), still held great appeal for many. Large residences dating from the first decade of the nineteenth century include: Ballycurry (1807), near Ashford *(fig. 62)*; Ballynure (c. 1800), Grange Con *(figs. 63-64)*; Castle Howard (1811), Avoca *(figs. 65-66)*; Cronybyrne House (c. 1800), Rathdrum; Donard House (1813), Donard; Glanmore Castle (c. 1800), near Ashford; and Tynte Park (c. 1835), Dunlavin. Older buildings such as Carnew Castle (c. 1590 and c. 1817), Carnew; Fortgranite (c. 1730 and c. 1815), Baltinglass *(fig. 67)*; Glenart Castle (c. 1820), Arklow; Glendalough House (c. 1750 and c. 1840), Annamoe; Kilruddery (c. 1650 and 1820), Bray; and Shelton Abbey (1770 and

(fig. 67)
FORTGRANITE HOUSE
Fortgranite
(c. 1730 and c. 1815)

Fortgranite's early eighteenth-century origins have been successfully disguised by the late Georgian application of a Classical portico and tall parapet.

(fig. 68)
DONARD HOUSE
Donard Demesne East,
Donard
(1813)

Donard House,
designed by William
Vierpyl, is typical of
the unassuming but
substantial gentry houses
which continued to be
built after the Union
(1800).

(fig. 69)
DONARD HOUSE
Donard Demesne East,
Donard

The rustic quality of
the outbuilding ranges,
achieved through the
use of coarsely-hewn
rubble stone, is in
marked contrast with
the refined elegance
of the main house.

(fig. 70)
GLENAIR HOUSE
Stilebawn,
Delgany
(c. 1830)

Relatively small single-storey or single-storey over basement country houses came into vogue in the Regency period. Veranda style porches were a feature common to many.

(fig. 71)
GLENBROOK HOUSE
Stilebawn,
Delgany
(c. 1800)

With its clean lines, sober façade and elegant door surround, Glenbrook is in many respects the archetypal late Georgian Irish gentleman's residence. The canted bays to the sides were added later in the century.

(fig. 72)
BRUNSWICK ROW
Main Street,
Carnew
(c. 1830)

Due in part to its relatively large size, the Fitzwilliam Estate in the south of the county became involved in numerous building projects. This particularly long estate workers' terrace at Carnew is one of the largest, containing, what were for the time, quite substantial two-storey dwellings, complete with rear outbuildings. Many of the properties were altered in the twentieth century, but the scale of the terrace still impresses.

1819) Arklow, were remodelled and extended around the same time. Some of these houses, Ballycurry, Ballynure, Cronybyrne House, and Donard House *(figs. 68-69)* for instance, follow forms derived from the neo-Classical. Others are enlivened with fashionable Regency touches such as porticoes, large decorative fanlights, bowed bays, and overhanging eaves. These forms and details, which remained influential in many quarters well into the 1840s, were particularly evident in the smaller houses of minor gentry and the town houses of the aspiring merchant and professional classes, all of whom prospered from the wartime boom. Glenair (c. 1830) *(fig. 70)* and Glenbrook (c. 1800) *(fig. 71)*, both near Delgany, represent two gentry villas of the period. The former utilises the single-storey over basement model, the latter is a square two-

storey building with a hipped roof. Both are relatively simple in terms of design and, in the case of Glenbrook, little different than the gentry dwellings of the second half of the previous century. However, as well as the distinctly Regency detailing, both have a fineness in their execution that is lacking in many similarly-sized houses of a generation or two earlier. Number 23 Lower Main Street (c. 1810), Arklow, is a particularly large and well preserved terraced town house of the same period with a finely, if eclectically, detailed door and shopfront *(fig. 73)*; again all very typical of the time. Something of the quality of Regency design is also evident in more modest dwellings of the period, as demonstrated by Brunswick Row (c. 1830), a lengthy terrace built by the Fitzwilliam estate at Carnew *(fig. 72)*.

(fig. 73)
23 MAIN STREET LOWER
Arklow
(c. 1810)

Largely intact early nine-teenth-century shopfronts are a very rare commodity. This property in Arklow possesses one of the finest examples in the county which dates to c. 1840.

RAYMOND GAFFNEY
10 Ferrybank,
Arklow
(c. 1845)

A pleasant shopfront dating to the late nineteenth century, incorporating elegant carved details.

**FITZWILLIAM SQUARE/
BRIDGE STREET
Wicklow
(c. 1800)**

A commercial space is carefully integrated into an existing house without adversely affecting the Classical harmony of the symmetrical design. The simple shopfront dates to the turn of the twentieth century.

**COMERFORD
Main Street,
Rathdrum
(c. 1810)**

A simple shopfront (c. 1885) conforms to a traditional Irish model, based on a symmetrical plan and featuring Classically-derived elements including panelled 'pilasters' and subtle decoratively-carved consoles.

**MAIN STREET
Dunlavin
(c. 1830)**

An attractive, simple timber shopfront dating to the mid nineteenth century, which has survived intact despite the conversion of the ground floor back to residential use.

(fig. 74)
CASTLE HOWARD
Castlehoward
(1811)

A complex design by Sir Richard Morrison sought to combine two elements of archaeologically-derived architecture, namely a stout fortified 'castle' block adjacent to which runs an abbey-like wing.

The clean lines inspired by Classical antiquity were not favoured exclusively at the turn of the century and new styles, which harked back to the Middle Ages, became increasingly prevalent from 1810 onwards. This revival of interest in the Gothic style was inspired primarily by the great cathedrals, castles, and manor houses of the medieval period as characterised by the use of pointed arch openings, gables, towers and pinnacles, all set within naturalistic landscapes. It was in many respects a product of the European Romantic movement which was to pervade art and literature in the latter years of the eighteenth and first half of the nineteenth century. As such, it was a style particularly suited to the dramatic and evocative landscape of Wicklow. It also appealed to the new found sensibilities of many of the county's lineage-conscious magnates, many of whom could not trace their Irish ancestry much beyond the later 1600s, and to whom a castellated pile suggested a link with a more distant past. Early attempts at medieval styling dating from the late 1700s usually involved what were in essence Classical symmetrical forms with castellated parapets, pinnacles or towers simply applied in a fanciful manner which owed little to historical accuracy. Altidore Castle (c. 1780–90), near Kilpedder, is a good example of this Gothick or 'toy fort' style, as is Glanmore Castle (1804), near Ashford. Castle Howard (1811), near Avoca, built to designs by Dublin architect Sir Richard Morrison (1767–1849) in 1811, is a step into the realms of truer medieval form *(figs. 74-75)*; an asymmetrical composition with a three-storey tower with round turrets and a two-storey 'abbey' wing. Shelton House (1770),

(fig. 75)
CASTLE HOWARD
Castlehoward

An engraving by J.P. Neale shortly following completion of the building programme somewhat exaggerates the Romantic setting of the surrounding landscape.

Courtesy of the Irish Architectural Archive.

KILCARRA HOUSE
Kilcarra West,
Woodenbridge
(1888)

A gateway and attendant lodge of eclectic appearance, displays the contemporary taste for the medieval and/or exotic, regardless of whether such details succeeded on a small scale.

(fig. 76)
FORTGRANITE HOUSE
Kilmurry
(c. 1830)

The Gothick or toy fort style proved a particularly popular choice in relation to smaller estate structures such as gateways and lodges.

(fig. 77)
FORTGRANITE HOUSE
Kilmurry

A small-scale building that is almost overwhelmed by robust Gothic dressings, the lodge provided basic but adequate accommodation for a worker on the Fortgranite House estate.

(fig. 78)
FORTGRANITE HOUSE
Fortgranite
(c. 1840)

Decorative details ranging from paired pointed-arch window openings to the scalloped bargeboards on the deeply overhanging eaves indicate the equal importance placed on the ornamental and functional qualities of estate-related buildings.

remodelled in 1819 by Morrison for William Forward Howard (1788-1869) the 4th Earl of Wicklow, is a serious attempt to apply the elements of the genre to an existing structure, even to the extent of renaming the mansion Shelton Abbey; however, for all its medieval pretensions, the mid-Georgian symmetry of the original building is still apparent. At Carnew Castle, a sixteenth-century tower house restored in 1817 by William Fitzwilliam (1748-1833) the 4th Earl Fitzwilliam, the process was reversed as the regular late Georgian fenestration was shoehorned into a less than regular structure. At Fortgranite, near Baltinglass, a grand castellated gateway (c. 1830), complete with towers, was added to the main drive *(figs. 76-78)*; the early eighteenth-century house (c. 1730), contrastingly, was remodelled (c. 1815) along simple Classical lines. The rather more domesticated Tudor and Elizabethan Revival styles ran parallel with other forms of Gothic from the 1820s onwards. These styles lacked the overtly militaristic details of castellations and towers, and placed greater emphasis on steeply pitched roofs, tall chimneystacks, decorative gables, bays, and mullioned and transomed windows. Kilruddery House (originally c. 1650), near Bray, extended and remodelled by the prolific Morrison for John Chambré Brabazon (1772-1851) the 10th Earl of Meath in the early 1820s, is possibly the finest of the slightly less angular Elizabethan variety in the whole of Ireland *(figs. 79-80)*. Glendalough House (c. 1750; remodelled, c. 1840), near Laragh, exemplifies the Tudor genre in the county. Significant portions of both houses were demolished in the 1900s but what has survived, particularly of Kilruddery, is still impressive.

(fig. 79)
KILRUDDERY HOUSE
Kilruddery
Demesne West,
Bray
(c. 1650 and 1820)

A seventeenth-century
house entirely remodelled
in the Elizabethan Revival
style for John Chambré
Brabrazon (1772-1851)
by Sir Richard Morrison.
The house was greatly
reduced in size in the
1950s following the
removal of a substantial
portion of the entrance
front. An elegant conser-
vatory was added in 1852
to the designs of William
Burn (1789-1870).

(fig. 80)
KILRUDDERY HOUSE
Kilruddery
Demesne West,
Bray

Formal gardens estab-
lished in the late seven-
teenth and early eigh-
teenth centuries have
been continuously devel-
oped over subsequent
centuries, and present an
impressive setting to
Kilruddery House.

(fig. 81)
THE CLOCK TOWER
The Square,
Enniskerry
(1843)

An imposing
Renaissance-style
clock tower, built as
a Wingfield family
memorial to designs
attributable to John
Louch (1797-1867),
forms the centrepiece
of the planned square at
Enniskerry. The cupola,
or dome, was added in
1860 by Sir George
Moyers (fl. 1860-84).

(fig. 82)
**POWERSCOURT
NATIONAL SCHOOL**
The Square,
Enniskerry
(1818)

Picturesque buildings,
such as this school
house, are a common
feature of the Wicklow
countryside, many
inspired, no doubt, by
the county's evocative
landscape.

LARAGH SCHOOL
Laragh East,
Laragh
(c. 1840)

An appealing, middle-
size school house con-
forming to an estab-
lished pattern that
accommodated a com-
mon entrance range
and flanking classroom
blocks in a symmetrical
design. The school is
now in residential use.

(fig. 83)
**ENNISKERRY GARDA
SÍOCHÁNA STATION**
Church Hill,
Enniskerry
(c. 1840)

Even the more
'institutional' buildings
at Enniskerry were
designed to enhance
the picturesque character
of the village, as this
former constabulary
barrack shows.

The Romantic notions which inspired the taste for Gothic and Tudor styles in the county's mansions were quickly adopted in buildings of a more modest nature, just as the Regency style had previously been popularised. Gables, steeply pitched roofs, tall chimneystacks, and mullioned and transomed windows, all derived largely from the Tudor style, were frequently mixed with purely decorative picturesque elements such as overhang-ing eaves with elaborate bargeboards and finials. In the village of Enniskerry, redeveloped by the Wingfields of Powerscourt after 1815, this picturesque mixture was used extensively *(fig. 81)*. The village school house (1818) *(fig. 82)*, constabulary barracks (c. 1840) *(fig. 83)*, inn (c. 1711 and c. 1835), almshouse (c. 1840), hall (c. 1850), and a large proportion of the houses both within and just outside of the settlement, are all built in this manner and

LISLEA HOUSE
Church Hill,
Enniskerry
(c. 1860)

One of a pair of houses
that are distinguished in
Enniskerry as the only
purpose-built nineteenth-
century semi-detached
residences in the locality.
Distinctive glazing pat-
terns, profiled timber joinery, and the many gables
add considerably to the
picturesque character of
the village.

(fig. 84)
BALLARD
Shillelagh
(c. 1840)

Though lacking the finery of many of the estate-designed structures at Enniskerry, the estate workers' houses at Shillelagh possess a simple charm which contributes much to the beauty of the village.

(fig. 85)
SHILLELAGH
(c. 1835)

One of a terrace of seven almost-identical estate workers' houses, the unrefined rubble stone construction of which presents an attractive textured effect in the street scene.

(fig. 86)
QUARRY STREET
Shillelagh
(c. 1860)

One of a group of sixteen semi-detached houses built by the Fitzwilliams as accommodation for workers on the Coolattin Park Estate.

(fig. 87)
COOLATTIN
(c. 1850)

The status of the more important, or more skilled, estate employees was reflected in dwellings they occupied, as this pair of substantial mid-nineteenth century semi-detached houses shows.

POLLAPHUCA BRIDGE
Blakestown
Lower/Britanstown
(c. 1820)

Designed by the Scottish engineer, Alexander Nimmo (1783-1832), this distinctive road bridge shows how, by the 1820s, 'medieval' styling was finding its way into all manner of structures.

Courtesy of the National Library of Ireland.

complement their well wooded, almost Alpine, surroundings. A picturesque, but much more rustic approach was adopted by the Fitzwilliam estate in Shillelagh, where two rows of simple two-storey cottages (c. 1840) in rubble stone with granite dressings were constructed *(figs. 84-85)*. Similarly rustic semi-detached single-storey houses (c. 1850) were built just to the north of the village at Quarry Street a few years later *(fig. 86)*.

Later, larger and more overtly Tudor-influenced designs appeared at Coolattin (c. 1850), another Fitzwilliam-owned village *(fig. 87)*. Such designs, exuding an air of rural tranquillity, helped to reinforce the idea of the benevolent landlord as well as blending in effortlessly with their surroundings, and giving an impression of age. As such, picturesque forms remained popular with Wicklow's landowners for years to come.

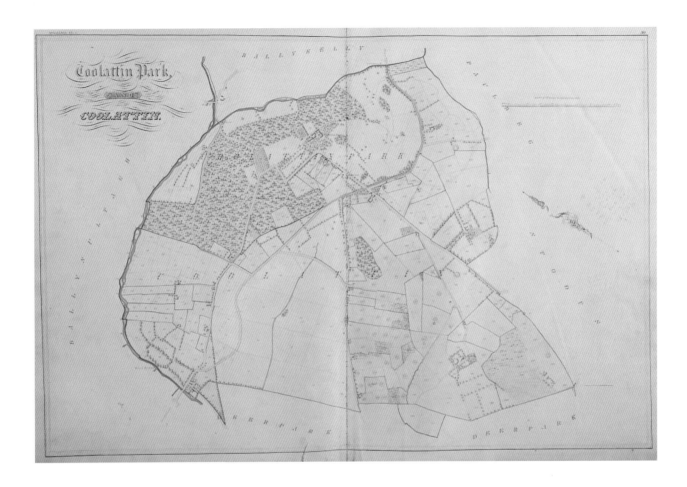

COOLATTIN PARK
Coolattin Park,
Shillelagh
(nineteenth century)

A nineteenth-century map demonstrates the Coolattin Park estate as expanded by the Fitzwilliam family in the eighteenth and nineteenth centuries. Various auxiliary buildings and features including a substantial wood are indicators of the development of the ancillary aspects of the grounds following completion of the improvements to the main house in 1801-04.

Courtesy of the National Library of Ireland.

COOLATTIN LODGE
Coolattin
(c. 1840)

A Classically-composed
estate manager's house
forms the centrepiece
of a farmyard complex
formally arranged on
a quadrangular plan
about a courtyard.

SHILLELAGH
COURTHOUSE
Ballard,
Shillelagh
(c. 1860)

A small-scale courthouse
forming the civic centre
of the village of
Shillelagh. Although now
apparently disused, the
building retains most of
its original character, and
contributes to the value
of the streetscape.

SHILLELAGH
COURTHOUSE
Ballard,
Shillelagh

A finely-detailed,
timber-clad clock tower
enlivens the roofline of
the courthouse and forms
a distinct focal point of
an otherwise simple
composition.

(fig. 88)
SHILLELAGH CHURCH
Ballard,
Shillelagh
(1834)

The quality of many Church of Ireland parish churches was to a large extent dictated by the means of the local landowner. The extensive Fitzwilliam estate in the south of the county, was able to supply the parishioners of Shillelagh with this particularly fine example, built in ashlar granite.

(fig. 89)
SHILLELAGH CHURCH
Ballard,
Shillelagh

A detail of the elegantly-appointed gateway allowing access on to the grounds of the church.

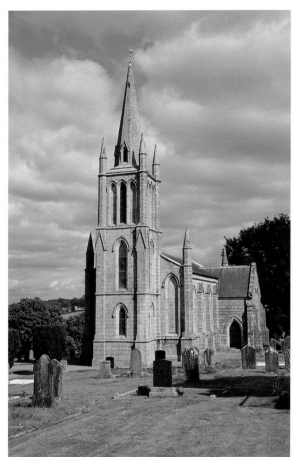

(fig. 90)
SAINT NICHOLAS'
CHURCH
Stephen Street,
Dunlavin
(1816)

An attractive middle-size church belonging to the Board of First Fruits group which is distinguished by the cut-stone battlemented entrance tower. Transepts were added in 1835, while the chancel was added in 1897.

Creating a visual link with the past was part of the reason for the widespread use of Gothic by both the Church of Ireland and the Roman Catholic Church during much of the nineteenth century. Both made claims to be the true inheritors of the medieval church and were to use their buildings to reinforce this impression. The Church of Ireland had embarked upon a programme of rebuilding in the early eighteenth century, a programme which had intensified in the late 1700s. In the face of the greater relaxation of the Penal Laws in the early 1800s, culminating with Emancipation in 1829, the church greatly increased its efforts, and the years between 1810 and 1840 witnessed an accelerated building programme. The vast majority of the county's many Protestant churches date from this

(fig. 91)
MOYNE CHURCH
Moyne
(1815)

A picturesque rural church, the setting quality of which is enhanced by the attendant grave-yard containing a fine collection of cut-stone markers.

(fig. 92)
SAINT JOHN'S CHURCH
Cloghleagh
(1834)

Before the more scholarly forms of Gothic became the main influence on Church of Ireland (and Roman Catholic) designs from the 1840s onwards, some churches adopted elements of the Gothick or 'toy fort' style.

(fig. 93)
ALL SAINTS CHURCH
Main Street,
Carnew
(c. 1860)

An imposing Tudor-style church of muscular appearance which represents the latest model on site. An adjacent slender tower survives as a remnant of an earlier church built in the previous century.

period and most followed the familiar nave and entrance tower plan structures, as seen at Donard (1835). The addition of chancels and transepts was also more common, with both featuring at Shillelagh (1834) *(figs. 88-89)*, and at Dunlavin (1816; enlarged 1835) *(fig. 90)*. Most of the churches built around this time are Gothic in terms of detail, but are by no means uniform in pattern. The churches at Dunlavin, Donard and Moyne (1815) *(fig. 91)* employ the Early English style, a largely pared down form of the genre with decoration mainly restricted to spiky pinnacles and battlements on the tower. Shillelagh, with its octagonal spire and pinnacles, is slightly more complex and shows tendencies towards the later Decorated style. Saint John's Church (1834), at Cloghleagh, mixes elements of Early English, Decorated, and Tudor styles *(fig. 92)*, while the nave of the church at Carnew (c. 1860) is largely Tudor in inspiration *(fig. 93)*.

(fig. 94)
SAINT PATRICK'S AND
SAINT KILLIAN'S
CATHOLIC CHURCH
Clara More,
Clara
(1799)

The decades between the beginning of the easing of the Penal Laws in the 1770s and Emancipation in 1829, showed a gradual increase in the number, prominence and scale of Roman Catholic churches. However, though the size of buildings may have increased, a relative lack of resources meant that most still followed the simple barn form.

(fig. 95)
SAINT JOSEPH'S
CATHOLIC CHURCH
Valleymount
(1803)

Existing churches that were remodelled following Emancipation were frequently brought up to date through the application of Gothic motifs. However, the frontage of Saint Joseph's (c. 1835) has no parallel in Ireland. The granite detailing is common to many churches in Wicklow and stands testament to the skills of local stone masons.

(fig. 96)
SAINT KEVIN'S
CATHOLIC CHURCH
Brockagh
Laragh,
(1846-49)

Saint Kevin's was built as a Famine relief project, supported by donations from local gentry, both Catholic and Protestant. Due to the circumstances of the times, the church, though relatively small, took over three years to complete.

(fig. 97)
SAINT JOSEPH'S
CATHOLIC CHURCH
Weavers Square,
Baltinglass
(c. 1860)

By the 1850s and 1860s Roman Catholic churches were rivalling their Church of Ireland counterparts in terms of scale and grandeur, particularly in urban areas. This example at Baltinglass was designed by John Bourke (d. 1871), the architect responsible for the Mater Misericordia Hospital in Dublin.

KNOCKANARRIGAN
PAROCHIAL HALL
Knockanarrigan
(1884)

A picturesque, small-scale building forming an attractive landmark in the small settlement of Knockanarrigan.

GLENEALY PAROCHIAL
SCHOOL
Ballymoat,
Gleaealy
(1867)

An attractive small-scale school of picturesque value forming a neat group with the associated Church of Ireland church built in the previous century (1792).

In the late eighteenth and early nineteenth century, the vast majority of Roman Catholic churches either followed the simple unadorned 'barn' form as typified by Saint Patrick's and Saint Killian's (1799), Clara Bridge, south of Laragh *(fig. 94)*, or the T-plan such as at the former church at Knockananna (1800) and Saint Kevin's (1830), Hollywood. Emancipation, the growing sense of confidence that followed, and the increasing wealth of its congregations meant that from the 1830s buildings were either remodelled along more elaborate lines or rebuilt altogether, almost exclusively along Gothic lines. Saint Joseph's Catholic Church (1803; remodelled c. 1835) at Valleymount had its front gable redesigned and an unusual flat parapet with outsized granite pinnacles added *(fig. 95)*. The inspiration behind this exotic façade is uncertain. One theory states that the priest responsible for it had spent time in Malta and wished to refashion his own church along the lines of the churches he had seen there. Another suggests that it was designed by some parishioners who

worked for a time in New Mexico – present day Texas! Hereafter Gothic predominated. Saint Kevin's Catholic Church (1846–49), Laragh, built to designs by the prolific James Joseph McCarthy (1817–82), was typical of the simple form, with a high pitched roof, buttresses and bellcote establishing a standard that many of the smaller rural Roman Catholic churches constructed from the 1840s onwards were to follow *(fig. 96)*. As the historically correct form of Saint Kevin's shows, McCarthy was keen to promote 'true' Gothic Revival principles in Ireland. Others followed his lead and, by the late 1850s, these principles had begun to pervade the buildings of both main denominations. This is particularly evident in those larger churches built in urban areas, like Saint Mary's Catholic Church (1859), Enniskerry, Saint Joseph's Catholic Church (1860), Baltinglass *(fig. 97)*, and Christ Church (1863), Bray. By this date many Roman Catholic churches were adopting a French Gothic style, but the other English-derived flavours were never totally excluded.

With the disestablishment of the Church of Ireland in 1869, its building programme decreased drastically throughout Ireland. Even in County Wicklow, where the percentage of Protestants was relatively high, there are few new church buildings from this period. Exceptions include Saint Mary's Church (1884), Baltinglass, and the impressive Saint Saviour's Church (1899), Arklow *(figs. 98-101)*. Saint Saviour's, designed by the London architect Sir Arthur Blomfield (1829–99) down to the interior fittings and furnishings, very finely demonstrates the taste of its patron William, 5th Lord Carysfort (1836-1909).

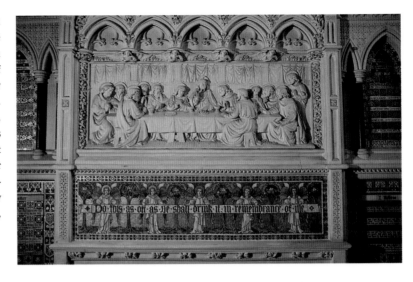

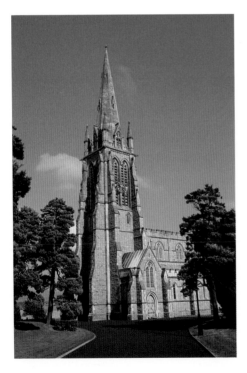

(fig. 98)
SAINT SAVIOUR'S CHURCH
Coolgreaney Road, Arklow
(1899)

Saint Saviour's, designed by the English architect Sir Arthur Blomfield (1829-99), is one of Wicklow's few post-Disestablishment Church of Ireland churches, and undoubtedly the most impressive. Blomfield, a keen exponent of the Gothic Revival style, was respected not only for his own compositions but also for his work as a restorer. The author, Thomas Hardy (1840-1928), who trained as an architect in his youth, was apprenticed to him for a short time.

(fig. 99)
SAINT SAVIOUR'S CHURCH
Coolgreaney Road, Arklow

A view of the nave and side aisles illustrating the stepped buttresses, battlemented parapets, and pinnacles that orchestrate the exterior of the Blomfield's scheme.

(fig. 100)
SAINT SAVIOUR'S CHURCH
Coolgreaney Road, Arklow

A well-preserved interior retaining most of the original furnishings includes a decoratively carved stone reredos depicting a tableau of The Last Supper.

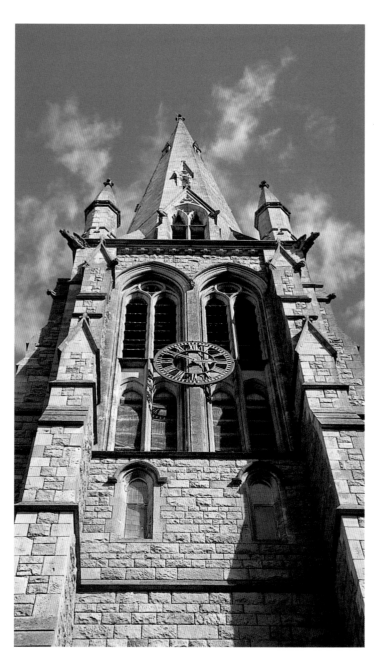

(fig. 101)
**SAINT SAVIOUR'S
CHURCH**
**Coolgreaney Road,
Arklow**

A detail of the upper
stages of the entrance
tower illustrating the various cut-stone dressings
and the polygonal spire
that presents a graceful
landmark in the skyline
of Arklow.

(fig. 102)
AVOCA COPPER AND
SULPHUR MINES
Ballymurtagh
(c. 1860)

Relics such as the disused
tram bridge illustrated
serve as a reminder of the
various elements of infra-
structure put in place in
the development of the
Avoca Copper and
Sulphur Mines.

(fig. 103)
AVOCA COPPER AND
SULPHUR MINES
Ballymurtagh
(c. 1850)

With copper extraction
commencing in 1720 and
continuing up until 1982,
Avoca has the longest
record production of any
Irish mine. An open iron
sulphide pit mined in the
1850s was, for a period,
reputed to be the largest
open pit in Europe.

The Victorian tendency to build churches and houses in styles which harked back to, in their view, more serene and socially stable medieval times, was in part a reaction to the rapid industrial and technological changes which were taking place around them. County Wicklow, like most of Ireland outside eastern Ulster, did not witness an industrial revolution on the scale of that which took place in Britain, but the few notable developments that did occur left their mark on the landscape. Perhaps the most spectacular of these took place in the Vale of Avoca, south of Rathdrum *(figs. 102-104)*. Iron mines in this area had been worked for centuries, and copper and silver had been mined since the early eighteenth century. By the 1840s the demand for sulphur by the emerging chemical industries in northwest England led to more intensive mining activity in the area, and by 1850 roughly two thousand mines were employed at Avoca, producing 140,000 tons of ore. As a result the by-then largely treeless vale became peppered with structures including winding engine houses with tall chimneys, stone built sheds, and tramlines. In the mid 1870s, in the face of cheaper ore imports from Spain, the mining operations at Avoca were drastically scaled down. By the early 1880s work on a significant scale had ceased. Trees have since reclaimed much of the old works, but chimneystacks, tramlines and bridges remain as an isolated and strangely evocative reminder of this one-time hive of industrial activity.

The granite quarries in the north east of the county were vibrant centres of industry in both the eighteenth and nineteenth centuries. The quarry at Golden Hill in the Parish of Kilbride had supplied the stone that was used to build Russborough House, as well as notable buildings in Dublin including the Custom House, the Four Courts, much of Trinity College, and the General Post Office. Supplies at Golden Hill became depleted by the 1820s and a new quarry was opened to the south at Ballyknockan. This quarry supplied granite for many more prominent Dublin buildings including three Roman Catholic churches: Saint Francis Xavier's, Gardiner Street; Saint Andrew's, Westland Row; and Saint Paul's, Arran Quay. Stone from the quarry at Ballyknockan was used too in many buildings throughout Wicklow itself, and also gave rise to a distinctive granite built village on its own doorstep.

(fig. 104)
GOLD MINES,
COUNTY OF
WICKLOW
(1804)

An engraving by J.
Bluck (fl. 1791-1819)
of London, dated 19th
May 1804, depicting
the operation of gold
mines that were once
an important natural
resource of the county.

*Courtesy of the
National Library of
Ireland.*

GOLD MINES, COUNTY of WICKLOW.

Many of the village's mid to late nineteenth-century buildings, originally occupied by the stonecutters who worked the quarry, still survive and many possess decorative granite embellishments. The aptly named Granite House (c. 1875), next to the quarry, possesses an extraordinary doorcase, described by Seán Rothery as 'a builder's catalogue of tricks in granite' *(fig. 105)*. Saint Anthony's (c. 1860), a smaller single-storey house to the north end of the village, possesses another striking, yet incongruous, granite doorcase, as well as a pair of distinctive gate posts with decorative finials.

Technological advance, rather than industrial activity, led to the rise of the much larger

(fig. 105)
GRANITE HOUSE
Ballyknockan
(c. 1875)

The Ballyknockan workers
were able to display their
craftsmanship through set
piece decoration to their
houses, as the doorway,
windows and gateposts of
Granite House show.

(fig. 106)
THE ESPLANADE
Strand Road,
Bray
(1859-61, 1886)

The completion of the first Esplanade in 1861 in many respects marked the arrival of Bray as a seaside resort. Prior to this the main focus of the town had been Main Street, with only a few small dwellings scattered along the seafront, fronting onto a narrow laneway next to the beach. By the early 1860s many of these had, or were about to be swept away to make room for large seafront terraces such as Brennan's, Royal Marine and Martello Terrace. The Esplanade was rebuilt in its present form in 1886.

Courtesy of the National Library of Ireland.

(fig. 107)
THE ESPLANADE
Strand Road,
Bray
(2004)

A present-day view of The Esplanade which remains a popular public amenity in the town.

settlement of Bray. Progress came in the form of the railway, which reached what was then a reasonably small and relatively unimportant market town in 1854. Almost immediately, it sparked off a building boom that transformed the town into a fashionable seaside resort, which was to enter the popular imagination as 'the Brighton of Ireland'. The handful of enterprising individuals central to this transformation included the railway engineer, William Dargan (1799–1867), and local businessman,

John Quin junior (d. 1869). Dargan laid out The Esplanade (1859–61) *(figs. 106-107)* while Quin supplied the land that allowed the Dublin and Wicklow Railway Company to lay out Quinsborough Road. Grand rows of houses were erected along these routes including Dargan [now Duncairn] Terrace (1859) *(fig. 108)*, Prince of Wales Terrace (1860–61) *(fig. 109)*, and Goldsmith Terrace (1863), all on Quinsborough Road, and all of which rivalled the town houses of Dublin. Prince of Wales

(fig. 106)
MARTELLO TERRACE
Strand Road,
Bray
(1860)

A group of eight houses forming an attractive element of the townscape of Bray. An intricate veranda embellishes the ground floor frontage and provides a balcony accessible from the first floor.

(fig. 109)
**PRINCE OF WALES
TERRACE**
Quinsborough Road,
Bray
(1861-63)

Directly facing Duncairn
Terrace, Prince of Wales
Terrace is undoubtedly
Bray's most sumptuous
residential development.
Its construction helped
transform a quiet, almost
semi-rural lane into a
grand thoroughfare, linking
the town's Main Street
with the recently opened
railway station.

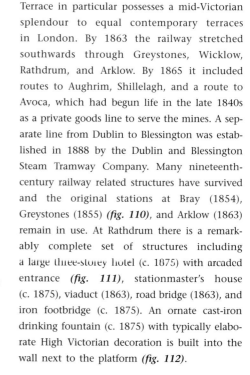

NEWCASTLE
RAILWAY STATION
Blackditch,
Newcastle
(1855)

One of a number of rail-
way stations constructed
during the development
of the Dublin and South
Eastern Railway line in the
mid nineteenth century.
Following closure in 1964
the station, like many
others across Ireland, was
successfully converted to
residential use.

(fig. 110)
GREYSTONES
RAILWAY STATION
Church Road,
Greystones
(1855)

Like Bray, Greystones
owes a large part of its
late nineteenth-century
expansion to the arrival of
the railway, with the focus
of development after 1855
shifting from the small
hamlet close to the coastline to the Church Road
area, leading directly to
the station itself.

(fig. 112)
RATHDRUM
RAILWAY STATION
Rathdrum
(c. 1875)

The popular image of
Victorian architecture
and design as one cat-
egorised by the appli-
cation of elaborate dec-
oration stems largely
from the 1860s and
1870s, when even the
most mundane objects,
such as this drinking
fountain, began to take
on a more ornate
appearance.

(fig. 111)
RATHDRUM
RAILWAY STATION
Rathdrum
(c. 1875)

Where local topography
dictated that a railway
station had to be set
a distance from an
established town or
village centre, it afforded
railway companies the
opportunity to offer pas-
sangers accommodation
in purpose-built hotels
such as this establish-
ment opened as the
Royal Fitzwilliam Hotel.

Terrace in particular possesses a mid-Victorian
splendour to equal contemporary terraces
in London. By 1863 the railway stretched
southwards through Greystones, Wicklow,
Rathdrum, and Arklow. By 1865 it included
routes to Aughrim, Shillelagh, and a route to
Avoca, which had begun life in the late 1840s
as a private goods line to serve the mines. A separate line from Dublin to Blessington was established in 1888 by the Dublin and Blessington
Steam Tramway Company. Many nineteenth-
century railway related structures have survived
and the original stations at Bray (1854),
Greystones (1855) *(fig. 110)*, and Arklow (1863)
remain in use. At Rathdrum there is a remarkably complete set of structures including
a large three-storey hotel (c. 1875) with arcaded
entrance *(fig. 111)*, stationmaster's house
(c. 1875), viaduct (1863), road bridge (1863), and
iron footbridge (c. 1875). An ornate cast-iron
drinking fountain (c. 1875) with typically elaborate High Victorian decoration is built into the
wall next to the platform *(fig. 112)*.

(fig. 113)
VARTRY TOWER
Vartry Reservoir,
Roundwood
(c. 1865)

Technological progress on a grand scale was a hallmark of the Victorian era. The rate of this progress, however, proved alarming to some contemporaries, and frequently new feats of engineering were disguised behind a 'traditional' façade. This draw-off tower is a good example of this, designed to resemble a relic from the Middle Ages.

The railways were not the only major feat of engineering that Wicklow was to witness in the 1860s; Vartry Reservoir was constructed by Dublin City engineer Parke Neville (1812–86) to supply the capital with a new source of water. Work commenced near the small village of Roundwood in late 1862. It required, amongst other things, the construction of a 1,640 foot long earthen embankment to act as a dam, with a draw-off tunnel underneath to accommodate the supply pipes stretching between the draw off tower (c. 1865) and the treatment works on the other side of the embankment. The draw-off tower itself is of particular architectural interest, built in the style of a medieval turret complete with castellations and pointed arch openings *(fig. 113)*. It is reached from the embankment by a contrasting iron girder bridge with twin latticed trusses with parabolic curved top chords. The bridge, incorporating the most up-to-date designs of the age, ironically gives access to a structure that attempts to resemble a building of centuries past. It is an ensemble which could almost be a metaphor for its time.

The Twentieth Century

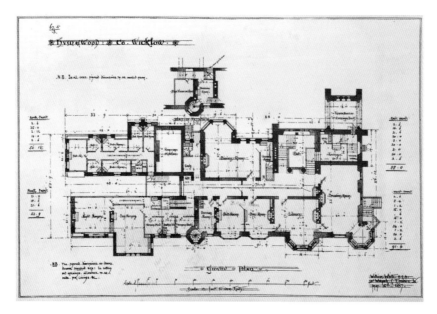

(fig. 114)
HUMEWOOD CASTLE
Humewood,
Kiltegan
(1867-70)

William Hume Dick MP (1805-92) is believed to have commissioned Humewood as 'an occasional resort in the summer or the shooting season'. Architect, William White (1825-1900), however, went beyond his original designs and exceeded his estimated expenditure of £15,000 by a then massive £10,000. The refusal to pay the difference to the builder, Albert Kimberly, resulted in a celebrated legal case: Kimberley v White and Dick. The builder won, and White's career was ruined in the process.

Courtesy of the Irish Architectural Archive.

The cataclysmic effects of the Great Famine (1845-9) and the high levels of emigration in the decades that followed saw Wicklow's population drop from 126,143 (1841) to 98,979 (1861), and then to 78,697 (1871). The loss of so many tenants meant a fall of income for the large estates and a consequent lack of means to support new building works. As a result, the boom in country house building which characterised much of the first half of the century, and indeed the century before that, tailed off almost completely. Humewood (1867-70), Kiltegan, a massive Gothic pile built for William Hume Dick (1805-92) to designs by eccentric English architect William White (1825–1900), was a notable exception *(figs. 114-123)*. Landlords also became inhibited by the rise of agrarian agitation, which led to the passing of successive Land Acts in the half century following 1870. The Land Acts were eventually to transform the landholding system from one of territorial landlordism to one of owner occupancy. These changes freed up land for development, particularly on the edges of the towns. Here the aspiring middle classes availed of the opportunity to erect a type of dwelling largely new to the county; the suburban villa. All of the country's larger urban areas were to witness this to a greater or lesser extent, but none so spectacularly as Greystones. Between 1890 and the outbreak of the First World War in 1914, a sizeable portion of the Burnaby Estate on the southern side of the town was taken up with a particularly dense development of such houses.

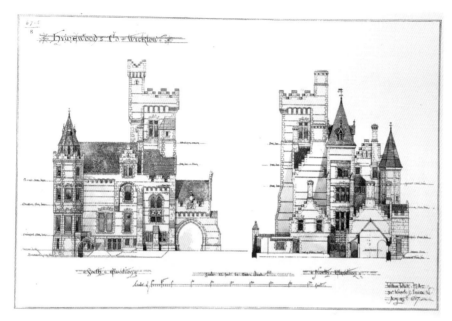

(fig. 115)
HUMEWOOD CASTLE
Humewood,
Kiltegan

An illuminated diagram exhibited by White to the Royal Institute of British Architects in 1869 illustrating the south (left) and north (right) frontages of the castle. The pyramidal massing of the main block, compromised by the later addition of a tower to the adjacent stable block, is readily apparent from these illustrations.

Courtesy of the Irish Architectural Archive.

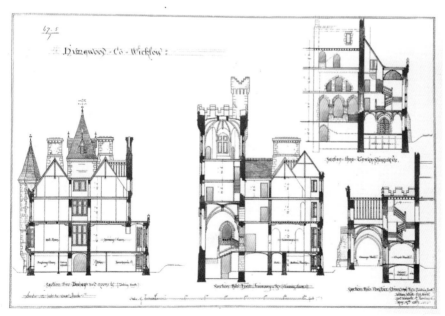

(fig. 116)
HUMEWOOD CASTLE
Humewood,
Kiltegan

Section drawings of Humewood Castle indicating the internal arrangement of, amongst others, the staircase hall.

Courtesy of the Irish Architectural Archive.

(fig. 117)
HUMEWOOD CASTLE
Humewood,
Kiltegan

The open porte cochère, soaring entrance tower, and polygonal corner turret are carefully coordinated to ensure that the viewer's gaze is constantly diverted and entertained on the approach to the house.

(fig. 118)
HUMEWOOD CASTLE
Humewood,
Kiltegan

A carved stone surround, intricate heraldic overpanels, and a groin-vaulted ceiling to the porte cochère are illustrative of the expert stone masonry that distinguishes Humewood Castle and which undoubtedly accounted for much of White's much-contested fee.

(fig. 119)
HUMEWOOD CASTLE
Humewood,
Kiltegan

A view of the south and west (or garden) fronts which, again, clearly illustrate the pyramidal massing of the main block as originally conceived by White.

(fig. 120)
HUMEWOOD CASTLE
Humewood,
Kiltegan

Finely carved details, including bas relief panels and trefoil-headed window surrounds provide intermittent light relief to the solid muscularity of the design.

(fig. 121)
HUMEWOOD CASTLE
Humewood,
Kiltegan

Solid masonry walls relieved by diminutive window openings and crow-stepped battlemented parapets compound the medieval fortified quality of the composition.

(fig. 122)
HUMEWOOD CASTLE
Humewood,
Kiltegan

Completed as part of an overall development of the Humewood estate, the stable complex is remarkably muted in quality and incorporates little of the excess witnessed in the main house.

(fig. 123)
HUMEWOOD CASTLE
Humewood,
Kiltegan

In contrast to the main house, subsidiary buildings throughout the estate, including the lodge pictured, reveal a restrained approach to the design, settling on refined details such as the canted bay windows for architectural distinction.

The middle classes, like the aristocracy and gentry of a century earlier, were keen that their new homes should reflect the latest architectural fashions. Among these were the designs based on English medieval vernacular forms, which had been promoted by William Morris (1834–96) and the Arts and Crafts Movement in Britain from the 1860s onwards. When translated to the Edwardian suburban villa, these forms evolved into what became known as the Domestic Revival style. This was marked by the use of asymmetric plan forms and large expanses of roofs, usually tiled. Tall chimneystacks, gables, dormers, and mullioned and transom framed windows were also typical, as were facades composed of a mixture of roughcast/peppledash, mock timber-framing and brick. Greystones contains several classic examples which utilise all or most of these elements, including the impressive Burleigh Lodge

(c. 1900), Portland Road; Glansheskin (1904), Whitshed Road *(fig. 124)*; Corrella (c. 1905), Saint Vincent's Road *(fig. 125)*; and Craglands (c. 1900), Portland Road *(fig. 126)*. However, although the Domestic Revival enjoyed considerable popularity in many quarters it was, by the first decade of the twentieth century, only one of a number of styles jostling for attention in the villa market. Among these, the eclectic Edwardian Freestyle mixed elements from various genres, such as profiled openings, mouldings, canted bays, and gables, in a single mass generally built of brick. Bray possesses some classic examples of this type in Edgewood and Glendair *(fig. 127)* (both c. 1907), King Edward Road, and Wellington House (c. 1905), Novara Avenue *(fig. 128)*. The latter combines elements reminiscent of both the Tudoresque and the Classical styles.

(fig. 124)
GLANSHESKIN HOUSE
Whitshed Road,
Greystones
(1904)

With its complex asymmetric plan, eclectic collection of bays and dormers, and sweeping red tile roof, Glansheskin is typical of the Domestic Revival style. Although inspired by English and Welsh medieval buildings the designs frequently went beyond 'traditional' bounds, with many owing just as much to the contemporary Free style, as the Middle Ages.

(fig. 125)
CORRELLA HOUSE
Saint Vincent's
Road/Whitshead Road,
Greystones
(c. 1905)

One of a number of
substantial houses built
on the partitioned
Burnaby estate at the turn
of the century, Corrella is
characterised by features
of the Edwardian period
including an irregular
plan, the combination of
a number of building
materials, and a varied
roofline.

(fig. 126)
CRAGLANDS HOUSE
Portland Road North,
Greystones
(c. 1900)

Mullioned window open-
ings framed by masonry
surrounds and featuring
leaded glazing patterns
suggest the influence of
English medieval vernacu-
lar forms on the appear-
ance of Craglands.

(fig. 127)
GLENDAIR HOUSE
King Edward Road,
Bray
(c. 1905)

An eclectic concoction of
canted and box bays, hips
and gables, and a construction almost entirely in
mass-produced red brick,
Glendair presents many
qualities that exemplify
the Edwardian period.

(fig. 128)
WELLINGTON HOUSE
Novara Avenue,
Bray
(c. 1905)

With its gables, mullioned
windows and brick façade
this house has a mildly
Tudoresque appearance.
However, in typical Free
style vein, the
composition has a
roguish canted bay,
vaguely Classical open
porch and a Renaissance-
style balustrade.

(fig. 129)
ALLIED IRISH BANK
Main Street,
Arklow
(1914)

The Queen Anne Revival long predates the Edwardian era, having begun in the late 1860s. The style is characterised by a lightness of appearance and details such as small-pane windows, dressings around and above openings, balconies, balustrades, overhanging eaves, and tall chimneys. Unlike the earlier Gothic Revival, it was not a scholarly revival, but blended elements in a way that laid the foundations for the later eclectic Free style.

(fig. 130)
BRAY POST OFFICE
Quinsborough Road,
Bray
(1904)

This building is typical of the Edwardian Free style, where elements of Classical architecture are applied without regard to the Palladian and neo-Classical ideals of symmetry, harmony and balance. Despite this dispensing with the rules, many such buildings have a liveliness and attractiveness which can add much to a streetscape.

This proliferation of styles and the lack of restriction on design pervaded many other classes of buildings as well as suburban dwellings. By 1914 financial institutions such as the bank (1914) in Arklow, now the Allied Irish Bank, had adopted exuberant neo-Queen Anne compositions, in this case complete with a robust Baroque decoration and an overhanging hipped roof *(fig. 129)*. The building stands in contrast to the nearby Bank of Ireland (c. 1880), built a generation earlier. This late Victorian institutional Italianate composition is much more sober, displaying a restrained rusticated granite ground level and unadorned red brick above. The freedom of stylistic expression is further illustrated by the post office (1904) in Quinsborough Road, Bray, where Queen Anne detailing has been applied to a typically Edwardian asymmetric form *(fig. 130)*. In the same spirit of diversity, the library (1911) in Enniskerry has a somewhat grand early Georgian doorcase fronting a rather small and homely single-storey building *(fig. 131)*. Although the library (1910) in Greystones displays a mixture of Queen Anne and early Georgian elements, the building is asymmetric,

like the post office on Quinsborough Road, and single-storey, like the library in Enniskerry *(figs. 132-133)*. The list of unrestrained design continues: the long terrace on the north side of Galtrim Road (c. 1907), Bray, combines Domestic Revival mock timber-framing with a Classically-inspired semicircular entrance to the recessed porch *(fig. 134)*. On nearby Adelaide Road a pair of similarly eclectic two-storey houses (c. 1910) sport particularly ebullient mock timber-framed jettied bays *(fig. 135)*. The joie de vivre displayed by the county's Edwardian architecture in many respects mirrors the political optimism of the time, when a peaceful transition to Home Rule for Ireland appeared a tangible possibility. These hopes were soon dashed. In the turbulent years that led up to Independence in 1922, and the uncertain years that followed, architectural flair by private individuals and by the state was, by and large, put on hold.

(fig. 131)
**ENNISKERRY CARNEGIE
FREE LIBRARY**
Church Road,
Enniskerry
(1911)

Originally intended to
be named Powerscourt
Library, this institution
was built as part of a
nationwide library build-
ing programme financed
by the Scottish-American
industrialist, Andrew
Carnegie (1835-1919).
The library at Enniskerry
was the work of R.M.
Butler (1872-1943), who
was also responsible for
libraries in towns as far-
flung as Dundrum,
County Dublin, Listowel,
County Kerry, and
Millstreet, County Cork.

(fig. 132)
**GREYSTONES CARNEGIE
FREE LIBRARY**
Church Road,
Greystones
(1910)

Like the library at Enniskerry,
this R.M. Butler composition
was originally symmetrical.
However, the balance was
upset in the 1940s when an
extension was added to the
north side.

(fig. 133)
**GREYSTONES CARNEGIE
FREE LIBRARY**
Church Road,
Greystones

A finely-detailed polygo-
nal vent topped with a
dome and weathervane
illustrates the attention
to detail that characteris-
es many Edwardian insti-
tutional buildings.

(fig. 134)
GALTRIM ROAD
Bray
(c. 1907)

The front façade of each
of the houses making up
this well-preserved terrace
is finished in a mixture of
brick, pebbledash and
painted render. Such a
combination of finishes
was common to many
Edwardian houses and
marked the start of a
trend which has been
employed in many subur-
ban housing develop-
ments ever since.

(fig. 135)
FERGUSLEA HOUSE
Adelaide Road,
Waverly Terrace,
Bray
(c. 1900)

The decoration at Ferguslea
is carried on through to
the garden gate and rail-
ings. During this period,
similar decoration would
usually have featured in the
interiors of houses, with
patterned tiling to vestibule
hallways, fire surrounds,
and embossed 'Anaglypta'
and 'Lincrusta' wallpapers.

(fig. 136)
SAINT KEVIN'S SQUARE
Main Street (off),
Bray
(c. 1930)

Faced with the onerous task of developing medium density housing schemes on a limited budget, it is unsurprising that each local authority placed greater emphasis on functionality over aesthetic aspirations. At Saint Kevin's Square bipartite window openings are an effective and economical means of establishing architectural individuality.

After 1922 the fledgling state, in common with many other emerging European democracies, took on the role previously occupied by many of the now defunct great estates and became involved in social building programmes. The state required both institutional buildings and, through local authorities, adequate homes for its citizens. To some extent some progress had been made prior to Independence, through new local authority housing schemes such as Saint Kevin's Square (c. 1930) in Bray *(fig. 136)* and the development of the national school system, which had been in operation since the 1830s. However, in the changed circumstances of the mid twentieth century the state's role greatly increased. Practicality was the order of the day and the form of the buildings was in many respects secondary to their function. Many new national schools for instance, such as those at Roundwood (1923) *(fig. 137)*, Aughrim (1934), and Blessington (1936) followed the somewhat functional and conservative single-storey gable-ended forms of their nineteenth-century

(fig. 137)
ROUNDWOOD
NATIONAL SCHOOL
Roundwood
(1923)

With its simple gable-ended form, 'Georgian' sash windows and plain façade, this school could easily be mistaken for an 1830s or 1840s building. However, it is typical of many village schools of the early twentieth century and indicates the common design source of the Board of Works or Office of Public Works.

predecessors. Enniskerry National School (1939-40) is an exception to the rule and is built in a style that leans more towards the Modern *(fig. 138)*. Garda Síochána stations also followed the same simple functional lines. The station at Aughrim (1943) was built using the Office of Public Work's popular neo-Georgian model, while that at Roundwood (1957) shows an even plainer neo-vernacular Georgian style *(fig. 139)*. In terms of housing, mid-century buildings with simple clean red brick lines and the provision of gardens were far in advance of anything which had gone before. This is particularly evident in local authority developments such as at Rory O'Connor Place (c. 1950), Arklow *(fig. 140)*. However, it is interesting to note that these houses appear to have originally been fitted with Georgian-style multiple-pane timber sash windows. One wonders whether this was simply an anachronism, or a conscious attempt to create a visual link with the past.

(fig. 138)
SAINT MARY'S AND SAINT GERARD'S NATIONAL SCHOOL
Church Road, Enniskerry
(1939-40)

This building departs from the relatively simple 'traditional' forms which remained prevalent in the design of rural-based national schools during the first half of the twentieth century. The use of granite, a traditional material, helps to tie the building in with its surroundings.

(fig. 139)
ROUNDWOOD GARDA SÍOCHÁNA STATION
Roundwood
(1957)

The building of the station at Roundwood was prompted by the fact that the residence of the then President, Sean T. O'Kelly (1882-1966), was situated close to the village.

(fig. 140)
RORY O'CONNOR PLACE
Arklow
(c. 1950)

The role of the state in providing adequate housing through local authority developments such as this resulted in an acceleration in the growth of towns such as Arklow from the mid 1900s onwards.

An attempt to break with the past, rather than emulate it, inspired the radical new designs of the Modernist movement, the influence of which began to be felt in some privately developed buildings from the 1930s onwards. Some of the county's earliest examples can be seen in Bray, among them Saint Canice (1937), Strand Road *(fig. 141)*, and Sunningdale (c. 1930) at the corner of Putland Road and Edward Road *(fig. 142)*. Both houses, having a stark angular building-block appearance with large picture windows and tall parapets, represent something of the Art Deco glamour of the era. However, for all of their Modernist sophistication, both have made concessions to their environment in that their tall parapets disguise decidedly traditional pitched roofs – a must considering the Irish weather! For a purer Modernist statement Wicklow had to wait for the Summerhouse (1972) designed, overlooking the River Dargle, for Sir Basil Goulding (b. 1909) *(figs. 143-144)*. The house, the work of Ronald Tallon (b. 1927), is a stark and angular steel-framed flat-roofed box structure supported on steel stilts with panels of glass and cedar wood cladding. Influenced by the work of Ludwig Mies van der Rohe (1886–1969) and Frank Lloyd Wright (1869–1959), it stretches out over the steep bank of the river and is at once dramatic and completely at home with its surroundings.

(fig. 141)
SAINT CANICE
Strand Road,
Bray
(1937)

Art Deco-inspired designs such as this proved particularly popular in coastal areas and seaside resorts throughout Ireland by the middle decades of the twentieth century.

(fig. 142)
SUNNINGDALE HOUSE
Putland Road/
Edward Road,
Bray
(c. 1930)

Despite its Modernist 'Art Deco' ambitions, the actual form of Sunningdale is not that far removed from earlier Edwardian and late Victorian houses in Bray. However, the large windows, tall stepped parapet and sparse detailing were a radical departure for housing in the town at the time.

(figs. 143-144)
GOULDING
SUMMERHOUSE
The Dargle Road,
Kilcrone
(1972)

The Goulding
Summerhouse is probably
the most memorable piece
of Modernist architect in
the whole of County
Wicklow. Although not on
the same scale, the building's clean angular form
and wooded riverbank
setting are reminiscent
of Falling Water in
Pennsylvania by Frank
Lloyd Wright
(1869-1959).

By the early twentieth century the building of places of worship for the Church of Ireland community had stagnated, although the building of Roman Catholic churches continued apace. However, each successive church followed relatively similar patterns that had origins in nineteenth-century fashions and it was not until 1962, when the Second Vatican Council reconsidered the restrictions on forms of worship, that each parish was allowed greater freedom of expression in the form and appearance of the churches themselves. Thus the design of church buildings became unfettered from the largely Gothic styling of the previous 130 years or so, and architects became free to express themselves with more daring compositions and new materials. Saint Feargal's Catholic Church (1980) at Ballywaltrim, near Bray, is possibly Wicklow's most outstanding example of the application of Modernism to church architecture, with the Catholic Church of Our Lady of the Most Holy Sacrament (1981) at Blessington another striking instance of the profound change which had been brought about since the 1960s *(fig. 145)*. Both buildings, by abandoning references to traditional church forms, help to facilitate the Vatican II concept of worship as a community celebration, and blur the divisions between the celebrant and the congregation.

Bray Civic Offices and the adjacent Mermaid Arts Centre (2002), a community focal point of a different kind, represent another application of Modernism into the public arena *(fig. 146)*. A product, in a sense, of the Celtic Tiger economy, the business-like clean lines, sweeping curves, and vast glazed frontage of the main Council office building stand in contrast to the half-timbered faux medievalism of the nearby former town hall (1884) *(fig. 147)*. The difference in styles could not be greater. The earlier structure, built by the then local landlord Reginald Brabazon (1841-1929) the 12th Earl of Meath, is a remnant of the county's oligarchic past, when major architectural projects were the work of a relatively small handful of wealthy estate owners. The new complex is a building which purports to represent no one person but a large body of citizenry. The originators of the two buildings represent something of a contrast, but the intention to impress through architecture, be that on the part of an individual or a much larger group, remains common to both.

(fig. 145)
CATHOLIC CHURCH OF OUR LADY OF THE MOST HOLY SACRAMENT
Main Street, Blessington
(1981)

Following the Second Vatican Council architects, for so long restricted to designing churches in 'traditional', mainly Gothic or Romanesque styles, could experiment with more unconventional forms. By the 1980s, in direct contrast to a generation earlier, churches were becoming the vanguards for Modernism and radical new design throughout rural Ireland.

(fig. 146)
BRAY CIVIC OFFICES
Main Street,
Bray
(2002)

The modernism of the
Civic Offices not only
provides a striking
contrast to the old town
hall of the 1880s, but
also to the largely nine-
teenth-century
streetscape of Bray.

(fig. 147)
BRAY TOWN HALL
Market Square,
Bray
(1884)

Funded solely by Lord
Brabazon, who wished 'to
do a benefit for the town
of Bray', the Town Hall
was initially a cause of
friction between the
patron and many of the
townspeople who viewed
the new building as 'costly in its decorations' and
'totally unsuited to the
needs of the town'.

BALLYMURRIN HOUSE
Ballymurrin Lower,
Kilbride
(c. 1675)

A late seventeenth-century
house substantially
extended in the following
century, and the evolution
of which is clearly
expressed in the massing
of the composition.

ROYAL NATIONAL
HOSPITAL
(FITZWILLIAM HOUSE)
Killadreenan,
Newcastle
(1894)

An impressive hospital in
a Queen Anne style built
to the designs of Sir
Thomas Newenham
Deane (1828-99).
Originally built as a sanatorium, the building
remains in use as a
healthcare establishment.

COOLGREANEY ROAD
Arklow
(c. 1910)

A small-scale house con-
structed using economic
mass-produced materials,
including corrugated-iron.
Profiled timber joinery
accents lend a refined
dignity to an otherwise
functional design.

AUGHRIM FLOUR MILL
Aughrim Lower,
Aughrim
(c. 1070)

A stout, rubble stone
industrial building that
was established as a
direct result of the com-
ing of the railway to the
locality: the mill was originally served by the
Shillelagh branch of the
Dublin and South East
railway line.

BLESSINGTON BRIDGE
Blessington
(c. 1935)

A stark concrete road
bridge of functional
appearance, incorporating
little extraneous architectural ornamentation,
forms a graceful feature
spanning the River Liffey.

Conclusion

The increase in population, together with a thriving economy and soaring house prices in Dublin city, have all led to immense pressure for development in the surrounding counties. This poses a potential threat to Wicklow's architectural heritage. Bray, Greystones, Wicklow, and Arklow, and the villages of Delgany, Enniskerry and Blessington have all been developed into satellite commuter towns of the Greater Dublin Area. If the county's architectural heritage is to be protected such development must be sensitively managed.

The architectural fabric of previous centuries is tangible evidence providing insight into the social, political and historical development of the county. Perhaps it is the understanding of this that has encouraged the conversion of old buildings to alternative uses. Glenart Castle (c. 1820), a large imposing nineteenth century country house, has been converted into a hotel, while the Wicklow Head Lighthouse (1778-81 and 1836), restored by the Landmark Trust in 1997, provides distinctive holiday accomadation. Work is ongoing to restore the former army barracks at Aughavannagh (1803) while the barracks at Glencree (1806) now functions as a reconciliation centre. All changes of use and restoration works to the courthouses at Avoca (c. 1870), Baltinglass (c. 1810) and Dunlavin (c. 1740) have been carried out with minimal loss of character. The great houses at Powerscourt (1731-40), Russborough (1741-52) and Avondale (1779) have found a new lease of life as popular visitor attractions.

As history is continuous, it will be necessary to examine and reassess the architecture of the twenty-first century, as the buildings of the present will in turn represent a legacy to the future.

Further Reading

Aalen, F.H.A., Whelan, Kevin, and Stout, Matthew, eds., *Atlas of the Irish Rural landscape* (Cork: Cork University Press, 1997)

Bence-Jones, Mark, *A Guide to Irish Country Houses* (London: Constable, 1988)

Brophy, Jim, and Flynn, Arthur, *The Book of Wicklow* (Bray: Kestrel Books, 1991)

Clare, Liam, *Victorian Bray A Town Adapts to Changing Times* (Dublin: Irish Academic Press, 1998)

Cox, R.C., and M.H. Gould, *Civil Engineering Heritage of Ireland* (Dublin, 1998)

County Wicklow Project, *The Emergence of Wicklow as a County 1606-1845* (1993)

Craig, Maurice, *Classic Irish Houses of the Middle Size* (London: Architectural Press, 1976).

Craig, Maurice, *The Architectural of Ireland from Earliest Times to 1880* (London: Batsford, Dublin: Eason, 1982)

Craig, Maurice, and The Knight of Glin, *Ireland Observed* (Dublin and Cork, 1980)

Cruickshank, Dan *A Guide to the Georgian Buildings of Britain and Ireland* (St Martin's Press, 1986)

Cruickshank, Dan, and Burton, Neil, *Life in the Georgian City* (London: Viking, 1990)

Danaher, Kevin, *Ireland's Traditional Houses* (Bord Fáilte, 1993)

Davies, K.M., *Irish Historic Towns Atlas, Bray* (Dublin: Royal Irish Academy, 1998)

de Breffny, Brian, and Ffolliot, Rosemary, *The Houses of Ireland* (London: Thames and Hudson, 1975)

Duffy, Sean, ed., *Atlas of Irish History* (Dublin: Gill and Macmillan, 1997)

Flannery, Judith, *Christ Church Delgany 1789-1990 Between the Mountains and the Sea* (1990)

Fletcher, Banister, *A History of Architecture on the Comparative Method* (Seventeenth edition, revised by R.A. Cordinley, London: The Athlone Press, University of London, 1961)

Flynn, Arthur, *History of Bray* (Cork and Dublin: The Mercier Press, 1986)

Flynn, Arthur, *History of County Wicklow* (Dublin: Gill & Macmillan, 2003)

Hannigan, K., and Nolan, W., eds., *Wicklow: History and Society* (Dublin: Geography Publications, 1994)

Irish Architectural Archive, *The Architecture of Richard Morrison, (1767-1849), and William Vitruvius Morrison, (1794-1838)* (Dublin, 1989)

Killanin, Lord, and Duignan, Michael V., *The Shell Guide to Ireland* (Revised and updated by Peter Harbinson, London, 1989)

Lawlor, Chris, *Canon Frederick Donovan's Dunlavin, A West Wicklow Village in the Late Nineteenth Century* (Dublin: Irish Academic Press, 2000)

Lewis, Samuel, *Topographical Dictionary of Ireland* (London, 1837)

Long, Bill, *Bright Light, White Water, The Story of Irish lighthouses and Their People* (Dublin, 1993)

Malins, Edward, and The Knight of Glin, *Lost Demesnes* (London, 1976)

O'Donnell, Ruan, *Exploring Wicklow's Rebel Past 1798-1803* (Wicklow '98 Committee, 1998)

O'Keefe, Peter, and Simington, Tom, *Irish Stone Bridges History and Heritage* (Dublin, 1991)

Ó Maitiú, Séamas,
and O'Reilly, Barry,
***Ballyknockan A Wicklow
Stonecutters' Village***
(Dublin: The Woodfield
Press, 1997)

O'Sullivan, John, Dunne, Tony,
and Cannon, Séamus, eds.,
The Book of Bray
(Dublin, 1989)

Reeves-Smyth, Terence, and
Michael Beazley,
Gardens of Ireland
(London, 2001)

Rothery, Seán,
***A Field Guide to the
Buildings of Ireland***
(Dublin: The Lilliput Press,
1997)

Rothery, Seán,
Everyday Buildings of Ireland
(Dublin, 1975)

Rothery, Seán,
***Ireland and
the New Architecture***
(Dublin: The Lilliput Press,
1997)

Shepherd, Ernie,
and Beesley, Gerry,
***The Dublin and South Eastern
Railway: An Illustrated History***
(1998)

HOLLYBROOK HOUSE
Hollybrook,
Bray
(1835)

A compact house in the
Tudor Revival style built
for Sir Robert Adair
Hodson (1802-31) to
designs prepared by
William Vitruvius Morrison
(1767-1849).

HOLLYBROOK HOUSE
Hollybrook,
Bray
(1835)

Paired elongated flues,
enriched with inscribed
patterns, lend a decora-
tive flourish to the
roofline at Hollybrook.

Registration Numbers

The structures mentioned in the text of this Introduction are listed below. It is possible to find more information on each structure by accessing our survey on the Internet at: **www.buildingsofireland.ie** *and searching by the Registration Number. Structures are listed by page number.*

02-03 Saint Saviour's Church, Coolgreaney Road, Arklow
16322001

03 Kilruddery House, Kilrudery Demesne West, Bray
16400816

03 Powerscourt House, Powerscourt Demesne, Enniskerry
16400717

03 Russborough House, Russborough
16400503

03 Dwyer-McAllister Cottage, Derrynamuck
16402801

06 Rathdrum Corn Mill, Low Street, Rathdrum
16318041

06 3 Vale Road, Arklow
16322002

06 Vartry Reservoir, Roundwood
16401801

06 Avoca Copper and Sulphur Mines, Ballymurtagh
16403508

07 Powerscourt House, Powerscourt Demesne, Enniskerry
16400717

08 Fort, Rathcoran
Not included in survey

08 Fort, Rathgall
Not included in survey

08 Saint Peter's and Saint Paul's Cathedral, Glendalough
Not included in survey

08 Saint Kevin's Kitchen, Glendalough
Not included in survey

08-09 Round Tower, Glendalough
Not included in survey

08 Vallis Salutis Abbey, Blessington
Not included in survey

09 Black Castle, Wicklow
Not included in survey

09 Bray Castle, Bray
Not included in survey

09 Kindlestown Castle, Kindlestown
Not included in survey

10-11 Kiltimon Castle, Dunran Demesne, Newcastle
16401904

10-11 Carnew Castle, Main Street, Carnew
16324015

10-11 Kilruddery House, Kilruddery Demesne West, Bray
16400816

10-11 Powerscourt House, Powerscourt Demesne, Enniskerry
16400717

10-11 Ballymurrin House, Ballymurrin Lower, Kilbride
16403107

12 Blessington House, Blessington Demesne, Blessington
Now gone

12 Saint Mary's Church, Market Square, Blessington
16303006

12 Mount Kennedy, Mount Kennedy Demesne, Newtown Mountkennedy
Not included in survey

12 Kilruddery House, Kilruddery Demesne West, Bray
16400816

12-13 Ballyarthur House, Ballanagh, Woodenbridge
16404003

13 Ballymoney House, Ballymoney, Kilbride
16403108

14-15 Clonmannan House (Old), Clonmannan
16402501

15 Tober House, Tober Demesne, Dunlavin
16401501

15 Hillbrook House, Carnew
Now gone

15 Kilmacurragh House, Westaston Demesne
16403005

16 Saundersgrove House, Saundersgrove, Stratford
16402116

16 Rosanna House, Rosanna Upper, Ashford
16402509

16-17 Clermont House, Newrath, Rathnew
16315007

18-25 Powerscourt House, Powerscourt Demesne, Enniskerry
16400717

19-25 Russborough House, Russborough
16400503

23 Gateway, Russborough House, Russborough
16400504

24-25 Shelton Abbey, Shelton Abbey, Arklow
16404005

25 Bellevue House, Delgany
Not included in survey

25 Ballyraheen House, Ballyraheen Crossroads, Ballyraheen
16404303

26-27 Avondale House, Avondale
16403007

27 Clonmannan House (New), Clonmannan
16402502

27 Mount Kennedy, Mount Kennedy Demesne, Newtown Mountkennedy
Not included in survey

28 Oldfort House, Newcastle Middle, Newcastle
16310016

28 Lodge, Newcastle Upper
16310018

28-29 Charleville House, Charleville Demesne, Enniskerry
16400713

30 Dunlavin Market House (Dunlavin Courthouse), Market Square/Main Street/Kilcullen Street, Dunlavin
16308001

30-31 House, Dublin Street, Stratford
16313005

31 Church of Saint John the Baptist, Church Street, Stratford
16313006

32 Wicklow Gaol, Kilmantin Hill, Wicklow
Not included in survey

32-33 Arklow Bridge, Arklow
16322046

32-33 Clara Bridge, Ballyhad Upper/Clarabeg South, Clara
16402411

34-35 Milestone, Hollywood Crossroads, Hollywood
16400910

34-35 Milestone, Kilranelagh House, Kilranelagh
16402719

34-35 Wicklow Head Lighthouse (New), Dunbur Head, Wicklow
16403101

36 Wicklow Head Lighthouse (Old), Dunbur Head, Wicklow
16403102

36 Saint Paul's Church, Main Street, Bray
16301290

36 Saint Kevin's Church, Knockroe, Hollywood
16400908

36-37 Saint Mary's Church, Market Square, Blessington
16303006

38-39 Christ Church, Delgany
16305026

38-39 Saint Saviour's Church, Main Street, Rathdrum
16318005

38-39 Saint Livinius Church, Church Hill, Wicklow
Not included in survey

39 Saint Michael's Church, Aghahold
Not included in survey

40-41 Boland's, 22 Main Street, Arklow
16322035

41 Ace Flooring, Main Street, Blessington
16303008

41 House, Newtown Mountkennedy
16307007

42 Hunter's House Hotel (Newrath Bridge Hotel), Ballinapark, Ashford
16402506

43 Downshire Hotel, Main Street, Blessington
16303013

44-45 Thatched Cottage, Delgany, Killincarrig
16304102

44 House, Moyne
16403304

44-45 Dwyer-McAllister Cottage, Derrynamuck
16402801

45 House, Donard
16311011

46-47 Glencree Reconciliation Centre (Glencree Military Barracks), Aurora, Glencree
16400203

46 Laragh Castle (Laragh Military Barracks), Laragh East, Laragh
16314007

46 Drumgoff Military Barracks, Drumgoff
Not included in survey

46 Leitrim Military Barracks, Glen of Imaal
Not included in survey

46 Aughavannagh Military Barracks, Aughavannagh
16402904

46 House, Moyne
16403304

48 Bray Martello Tower, Strand Road, Bray
16301084

49-53 Ballycurry House, Ballycurry Demesne, Ashford
16401907

49-53 Ballynure House, Ballynure Demesne, Grange Con
16402004

50 Castle Howard, Castlehoward
16403502

50 Fortgranite House, Fortgranite
16402708

50-53 Cronybyrne House, Cronybyrne Demesne
16402410

50-53 Donard House, Donard Demesne East, Donard
16311016

50 Glanmore Castle, Ballymaghroe
16402401

50 Tynte Park, Loughmogue Upper
16401503

50 Carnew Castle, Main Street, Carnew
16324015

50 Glenart Castle Hotel, Glenart, Arklow
16404001

50 Glendalough House, Drummin, Annamoe
16401810

50 Kilruddery House, Kilruddery Demesne West, Bray
16400816

52-53 Glenair House, Stilebawn, Delgany
16305021

52-53 Glenbrook House, Stilebawn, Delgany
16305023

53 Shelton Abbey, Shelton Abbey, Arklow
16404005

53 Brunswick Road, Main Street, Carnew
16324001

53-54 23 Lower Main Street, Arklow
16322043

54 Raymond Gaffney and Sons, 10 Ferrybank, Arklow
16322076

54 Comerford, Main Street, Rathdrum
16318023

55 House, Fitzwilliam Square/Bridge Street, Wicklow
Not included in survey

55 House, Main Street, Dunlavin
16308010

56-57 Castle Howard, Castle Howard
16403502

56 Altidore Castle (Altidore Sanatorium), Altidore Demesne, Kilpedder
16401201

56-58 Shelton Abbey, Shelton Abbey, Arklow
16404005

56 Glanmore Castle, Ballymaghroe
16402401

57 Kilcarra House, Kilcarra West Woodenbridge
16404002

58 Fortgranite House, Fortgranite
16402708

58 Gateway and Gate Lodge, Fortgranite House, Kilmurry
16402709

58 Estate Worker's House, Fortgranite House, Fortgranite
16402710

58 Carnew Castle, Main Street, Carnew
16324015

58-59 Kilruddery House, Kilruddery Demesne West, Bray
16400816

58 Glendalough House, Drummin, Annamoe
16401810

60 The Clock Tower, The Square, Enniskerry
16302001

60 Powerscourt National School, The Square, Enniskerry
16302031

60 Laragh School, Laragh East, Laragh
16314004

60 Enniskerry Garda Síochána Station, Church Hill, Enniskerry
16302048

60 Powerscourt Arms Hotel, The Square, Enniskerry
16302029

60 Enniskerry Parochial Hall, The Square, Enniskerry
16302003

60-61 Lislea House, Church Hill, Enniskerry
16302035

62-63 Estate Worker's House, Ballard, Shillelagh
16323011

84-85 Rosslea House, Waverly Terrace, Adelaide Road, Bray
16301139

86 Saint Kevin's Square, Main Street (off), Bray
16301280 - 1

86 Roundwood National School, Roundwood
16309006

86 Aughrim National School, Aughrim
16320025

86 Blessington National School, Main Street (off), Blessington
16303021

87 Saint Mary's and Saint Gerard's National School, Church Road, Enniskerry
16302016

87 Aughrim Garda Síochána Station, Aughrim
Not included in survey

87 Roundwood Garda Síochána Station, Roundwood
16309004

87 51 Rory O'Connor Place, Arklow
16322055

88 Saint Canice, Strand Road, Bray
16301085

88 Sunningdale House, Putland Road/Edward Road, Bray
16301021

88-89 Goulding Summerhouse, The Dargle Road, Kilcroney
16400724

90 Saint Fergal's Catholic Church (Ballywaltrim), Killarney Road, Bray
16400813

90 Catholic Church of Our Lady of the Most Holy Sacrament, Main Street, Blessington
16303011

90-91 Bray Civic Offices, Main Street, Bray
16301322

90-91 Bray Town Hall, Market Square, Bray
16301068

92 Ballymurrin House, Ballymurrin Lower, Kilbride
16403107

92 Aughrim Flour Mill, Aughrim Lower, Aughrim
16320023

92 Royal National Hospital (Fitzwilliam House), Killadreenan, Newcastle
16401901

92 House, Coolgreaney Road, Arklow
16322010

92 Blessington Bridge, Blessington
16303027

93 Greystones Harbour, Greystones
Not included in survey

93 Glenart Castle Hotel, Glenart, Arklow
16404001

93 Arklow Lighthouse (Old), Dunbur Head, Wicklow
16403102

93 Aughavannagh Military Barracks, Aughavannagh
16402904

93 Glencree Reconciliation Centre (Glencree Military Barracks), Aurora, Glencree
16404203

93 Avoca Courthouse, Main Street, Avoca
16403514

93 Baltinglass Courthouse, Market Square, Baltinglass
16316007

93 Dunlavin Market House (Dunlavin Courthouse), Market Square/Main Street/Kilcullen Street, Dunlavin
16308001

93 Powerscourt House, Powerscourt Demense, Enniskerry
16400717

93 Russborough House, Russborough
16400503

93 Avondale House, Avondale
16403007

95 Hollybrook House, Hollybrook, Bray
16400706

99 Struan Hill, Stilebawn, Delgany
16305022

101 Kilruddery House, Kilruddery Demesne West, Bray
16400816

102 Tinode House, Moanaspick
16400101

STRUAN HILL
Stilebawn,
Delgany
(c. 1830)

An elegantly-composed substantial late Georgian house that is set apart by the distinctive massing of a slender three-storey central block with two-storey flanking end bays.

Acknowledgements

NIAH

Senior Architect Willy Cumming
Survey Controller Flora O'Mahony
Survey Managers Erika Sjöberg and Marc Ritchie
GIS Technician Gareth John
Additional NIAH Staff Damian Murphy, TJ
O'Meara, Mildred Dunne and Barry O'Reilly

***The NIAH gratefully acknowledges the assistance
of the following in the preparation of the
Wicklow County Survey and Introduction:***

Survey Fieldwork
Paul Logan Architects

Recorders
Paul Logan, Philip Smith, Malachy McGowan and
John Logan

Introduction
Writer Philip Smith
Copy Editor Eleanor Flegg
Photographer Patrick Donald
Designed by Bennis Design
Printed by New Oceans

The NIAH wishes to thank all of those who
allowed access on to their property for the purpose
of the Wicklow County Survey and subsequent
photography.

The NIAH also wishes to acknowledge the gener-
ous assistance given by the staff of the Irish
Architectural Archive (IAA), the Mills and Millers
Society of Ireland, the National Library of Ireland
(NLI), the National Gallery of Ireland (NGI), the
National Photographic Archive, Coillte, and the
Knight of Glin for allowing the reproduction of a
photograph from his collections. The co-operation
of the staff of Wicklow County Council, in particular Heritage Officer Deirdre Burns, is also very
much appreciated. Thanks also to David Smith
who provided support to the Recording Team.

Sources of Illustrations

All of the original photographs for the Introduction
were taken by Patrick Donald. The illustrations listed below are identified by their figure number:

9, 10, 11, 18, 39, 45, 54, 57, 62, 67, 74, 86, 90,
92, 113, 118, 124, 126, 136, 139, and 141 taken
by Paul Logan Architects; 104, 106, and archival
images on pages 4, 20, 34, 63, and 64 are the property of the National Library of Ireland (NLI) and
have been reproduced with the permission of the
Council of Trustees of the National Library of
Ireland (NLI); archival image on page 7 courtesy
of Yale Center for British Art, Paul Melon
Collection, USA/Bridgeman Art Library; image on
page 9 courtesy of the photographic unit of the
Department of the Environment, Heritage and
Local Government; 15, 23, 34, 75, 114, 115, 116
courtesy of the Architectural Archive (IAA); 7
reproduced courtesy of the Irish Architectural
Archive and © the Knight of Glin; 22 and 23 courtesy of the National Gallery of Ireland (NGI); 40
courtesy of Trinity College, Dublin.

The NIAH has made every effort to source and
acknowledge the owners of all of the archival illustrations included in this Introduction. The NIAH
apologises for any omissions made, and would be
happy to include such acknowledgements in
future issues of this Introduction.

Please note that the majority of the structures
included in the Wicklow County Survey are
privately owned and are therefore not open
to the public.

ISBN: 0755719107
© *Government of Ireland 2004.*

KILRUDDERY HOUSE
Kilruddery
Demesne West,
Bray
(c. 1650 and 1820)

A detail of the Italianate conservatory added in 1852 by William Burn (1789-1870), designed to house both tropical plants and the Brabazon family's collection of statuary.

TINODE HOUSE
Moanaspick
(1864)

A detail of the highly
enriched iron gates that
serve as an elaborate
entrance on to the
grounds of Tinode House.

Questionnaire

Name:

Address:

Email:

Age: 10 - 18   18 -30   30 - 50   50 - 65   65+

Occupation:

Did you purchase this publication for: General interest   Professional use

Comments/Suggestions/Corrections:

The information in this questionnaire is to provide a feedback to the NIAH.
It will be kept confidential and will not given to any other authority.

The NIAH survey of the architectural heritage of County Wicklow can be accessed on the internet at: ***www.buildingsofireland.ie*** The data accessible on the internet includes a written record and images of each of the sites included in the NIAH survey. However, the mapping data, indicating the location of each site surveyed, is not available on the NIAH website.

If you would like to receive the mapping on CD-ROM please complete this questionnaire and send it with a stamped addressed envelope, large enough to hold a CD, to NIAH, Dún Scéine, Harcourt Lane, Dublin 2.